Praise for *Seaworthy* by Linda Greenlaw

"Book readers should rejoice. . . . Greenlaw's writing sweeps the reader along not only for the incidents at sea but also for her candid reflections about them. Her book won't make many landlubbers jump up and sign on for that kind of adventure. But they'll be delighted to have ridden along with her from the safety of their armchairs."
—*The Huffington Post*

"From mishaps to fish tales, Greenlaw keeps her narrative suspenseful. Between bad luck and self-doubt, she moves from experience to wisdom, guiding both crew and readers on a voyage of self-affirmation."
—*Publishers Weekly*

"Greenlaw speaks with unquestionable authority when fashioning the salty atmosphere of swordfishing life. A vanishing slice of life caught with ardor and freshness."
—*Kirkus Reviews*

"Greenlaw knows how to spin a good yarn. . . . *Seaworthy* is a more reflective book, pondering not just the vagaries of nature but the nature of success and self-definition."
—NPR.com

"Greenlaw is a remarkable woman who can hold her own, whether it's in the male dominated fishing industry or on the printed page."
—TucsonCitizen.com

"If *Seaworthy* is any indication, Linda Greenlaw's need to return to swordfishing is very real after all, and her careers as fisherman and bestselling author are far from over."
—OregonLive.com

"Pure joy."
—*The Florida Times-Union* (Jacksonville)

"Even if you never really wanted to go to sea for months at a time on a fishing boat . . . you'll be caught from the very first sentence of this engrossing and illuminating book."
—*San Francisco Book Review*

ABOUT THE AUTHOR

Linda Greenlaw, America's only female swordfish boat captain, lives on Isle au Haut, Maine. She was featured in the book and film *The Perfect Storm* and in the Discovery Channel series *Swords: Life on the Line*. She has written three *New York Times* bestselling nonfiction books about life as a commercial fisherman and two mysteries, and she has coauthored a cookbook with her mother, Martha Greenlaw.

Seaworthy

A Swordboat Captain Returns to the Sea

Linda Greenlaw

PENGUIN BOOKS

PENGUIN BOOKS

Published by the Penguin Group

Penguin Group (USA) Inc., 375 Hudson Street, New York, New York 10014, U.S.A.
Penguin Group (Canada), 90 Eglinton Avenue East, Suite 700, Toronto, Ontario,
Canada M4P 2Y3 (a division of Pearson Penguin Canada Inc.)
Penguin Books Ltd, 80 Strand, London WC2R 0RL, England
Penguin Ireland, 25 St. Stephen's Green, Dublin 2, Ireland (a division of Penguin Books Ltd)
Penguin Books Australia Ltd, 250 Camberwell Road, Camberwell, Victoria 3124,
Australia (a division of Pearson Australia Group Pty Ltd)
Penguin Books India Pvt Ltd, 11 Community Centre, Panchsheel Park, New Delhi–110 017, India
Penguin Group (NZ), 67 Apollo Drive, Rosedale, Auckland, 0632,
New Zealand (a division of Pearson New Zealand Ltd)
Penguin Books (South Africa) (Pty) Ltd, 24 Sturdee Avenue,
Rosebank, Johannesburg 2196, South Africa

Penguin Books Ltd, Registered Offices: 80 Strand, London WC2R 0RL, England

First published in the United States of America by Viking Penguin,
a member of Penguin Group (USA) Inc. 2010
Published in Penguin Books 2011

1 3 5 7 9 10 8 6 4 2

Map by Jeffrey L. Ward

THE LIBRARY OF CONGRESS HAS CATALOGED THE HARDCOVER EDITION AS FOLLOWS:
Greenlaw, Linda, 1960–
Seaworthy : a swordboat captain returns to the sea / Linda Greenlaw.
p. cm.
ISBN 978-0-670-02192-5 (hc.)
ISBN 978-0-14-311956-2 (pbk.)
1. Greenlaw, Linda, 1960– 2. Swordfish fishing—Grand Banks of Newfoundland.
3. Seafaring life—Grand Banks of Newfoundland. 4.Women ship captains—Grand Banks of
Newfoundland—Biography. 5. Ship captains—Grand Banks of Newfoundland—Biography.
6. Seahawk (Fishing boat) 7. Grand Banks of Newfoundland—Description and travel. I. Title.
SH691.S8G6895 2010
639.2'778—dc22 [B] 2009050233

Printed in the United States of America
Set in Warnock Pro · Designed by Amy Hill

This book is dedicated to
the hardworking men of the Seahawk:
Arthur Jost, Tim Palmer, Dave Hiltz,
Mike Machado, and Nate Clark.

Contents

Seaworthy

Prologue

The cell door closed with the mechanical, steely sound of permanence. I stood, hands in pockets, and stared through the small rectangular window as the officer's pale, stern face momentarily filled the glass slot. A hand appeared and slid the shutter closed, cutting off my last, tenuous tie to the outside world of statements, processing, and legal procedure. Had they really taken my belt and shoelaces? Sure, this was not my best moment. But sitting in a holding pen in Newfoundland, I hadn't actually considered suicide. On many occasions throughout my career, I had heard people refer to being at sea aboard a small vessel as analogous to being imprisoned. I, however, had always felt that being out on open water gave me a sense of freedom and liberation. My first experience inside a jail cell confirmed that for me a boat is a boat, prison is prison, and the two have nothing in common.

I was so distraught during the processing that when the officer who was emptying my bag and inventorying its contents asked a co-worker how to best categorize feminine products, it hadn't even registered. Normally I would have died from embarrassment. Hadn't they ever run a woman through the system before? Of course they had, I knew. I had watched the parade of reprobates, all tethered together, shuffle by and into a cell, and I was discreetly informed that "Friday is drunk day." There had been at least two, if not three, women in that lineup. I had looked away quickly, ashamed to have been caught checking them out. I wondered if they wondered, as I did about them, why I was here. So this is what true humiliation feels like, I thought.

A lot of head shaking, shoulder shrugging, and general disbelief had turned to hard, cold reality with the closing of that cell door. "Clink" and "slammer" were both appropriate synonyms, I realized, for a noisy entrance. Now the silence was remarkable. I missed the drone of the diesel engines and the squawking of the gulls. I took a deep breath and forced myself to turn away from the now-shuttered peephole and face my new surroundings. Alone. All alone. I like the feeling of solitude aboard a boat, I guess because I choose it. Being alone at sea was nothing like this. Perhaps being alone with my guilt was worse than rock bottom.

The cell was actually bigger than I had ever imagined one might be, especially a single. Not that I'd ever spent much time contemplating such things, but just in general I was surprised. The walls were white, as was the high ceiling, except for a few dried splatters of something I couldn't perceive as anything other than the semidigested contents of someone's stomach. I couldn't count the times I'd been hit in the face with spew when a seasick shipmate forgot about the wind. I'd always wiped it off with the back of my glove and never even blinked. Now I had to swallow what kept rising in my throat. The floor of the cell was a grayish color that I supposed was recommended for not showing grime. Overall, the cell was not actually clean. Sterilized was more like it. The smell of bleach evoked the image of a high-powered hose deployed on a weekly basis, but not a nice sweet smell like that of a freshly bleached fish hold.

There were a number of names and phrases strung together with four-letter words scratched into the walls and the bench seat that ran the length of the wall opposite the door. Fishermen often did similar scrawling on the underside of the bunk above them. I wondered how the inmates before me had etched the paint down to bare metal. And what for tools? Fingernails? Mine had been gnawed to nearly bleeding in the nerve-racked forty-eight hours since my arrest. And, I realized as I sat in the corner where the hard bench met the cold wall, I was too despondent to lash out even if I could.

Cooperative—that's what the arresting officers had said about me. Well, why wouldn't I be? I'm a nice girl. And I was totally and solely responsible for, and 100 percent guilty of, the charges on which I was now detained. And to top it all off, I was feeling too defeated to put up a fight anyhow. Should I have stood up to the three heavily armed and bulletproofed men who had boarded my vessel to investigate? At five foot three and 125 pounds, I think not. Should I have cut and run from the two-hundred-foot, state-of-the-art Canadian coast guard ship that had escorted me and my crew the 280 miles from the fishing grounds? Aboard the sixty-three-foot, six-and-a-half-knot jalopy of a boat called the

Seahawk, we had no chance. Maybe I should have protested. Now I felt like an absolute patsy. I sat on the bench, stared at the cell door, and quickly fell to a depth of despair that I never knew existed. I was well beyond tears. How could I have been so stupid? It's a long story. But I have time.

I'm Linda Greenlaw, the woman who was launched from near obscurity into a full fifteen minutes on the other end of the spectrum with the publication of Sebastian Junger's book *The Perfect Storm.* Being touted as one of the best swordfish skippers on the entire East Coast was a tough image for me to uphold at the close of a nineteen-year career full of the fits and starts that define commercial fishing. But I managed to make my uneasy peace with that mega image well enough. I retired from longline offshore fishing at the top of my game ten years ago. Since then I have been fulfilling a childhood dream of living year-round on Isle au Haut—an island in Penobscot Bay in Maine—where I reside today. The decade following my coming ashore from blue-water fishing is an example of real and drastic life change. Although hauling lobster traps had kept me on the water between the writing and promoting of six books during that span, small-boat fishing on the inshore waters surrounding my home did little to fill the void left in the absence of true, hardy saltwater adventure.

A bit hardier and saltier than I had hoped for so far, this latest adventure was still in its infancy when I landed in jail. Indeed, I had let my crew down. How and when would I explain this to my parents? And Simon? And what about Sarai? Not even a full year into my responsibility as legal guardian to the sixteen-year-old girl, and there I was in jail. What would Maine's Department of Health and Human Services think about that? I wasn't looking

like the ideal role model right now. Unfit at best. I had let everyone down, especially me. Pitying oneself is the most pathetic of
all pathetic indulgences in the human psyche. It's even worse than
hating oneself. And I had a lot of that going on, too.

I'd been given neither advice nor instruction from the arresting and processing officers. They must have assumed, wrongly,
that I had prior arrests and experience in this realm. I actually had
no idea how to act, what to say, or what not to say. My acquaintance with jail was limited to vicarious travels through stories told
by crew members. This was certainly the end of the prison intrigue
I had enjoyed toying with through the years. Not knowing how
long I would be locked up, I had nothing to do but sit and reflect
on how I'd come to this sorry state and wonder how soon it would
be before I got back offshore.

CHAPTER 1

The Call

I t had been a tedious, discouraging day of hauling lobster traps. My string of gear had been neglected, by both me and the lobsters, during a six-week stint of book touring, and the warps bore the telltale signs of inattention. These are the lines that stretch from buoys to traps, and mine were downright turfy with slime, sea-grass growth, and what could have been mistaken for the beginnings of a mussel aquaculture project. The catch was so pathetic I could see the bottom of the blue plastic barrel through the lobsters it contained at the end of the haul. With the price of bait and fuel soaring to an all-time high, it didn't take much math to figure that I was falling behind at a record pace. Disheartened, I threw a couple of buckets of water across the deck of the *Mattie Belle*, put her on the mooring, and headed home.

The bed of my pickup truck had finally slouched toward the

road far enough to rub against the axle or the driveshaft or something else it wasn't designed to ride on. All the structural-steel
components underneath were pretty well shot at this point, and
even the wooden block that the island mechanic, Ed White, had
jury-rigged had seemingly worn through. The Dodge Ram's 1983
body had been drooping for a while. But I had coaxed it along
gingerly all summer, hoping to get one more season of service
before coasting her onto a barge headed off-island and to wherever
the junks end up once they finally die. I eased over the last couple
of potholes, praying I'd reach my parking spot and avoid having
to abandon the wreck of a vehicle in the middle of my own drive-
way. I crept up a slight incline, swung into the shade of a stand of
spruce trees, and was relieved to stop and put an end to the awful
noise that the truck's most recent malady had produced.

Looking forward to a hot shower, I reached through the open
window of my truck and released the door from the outside, as the
latch no longer functioned from within, and stepped out of the
sagging pickup. As I approached the house, the front door flew
open and my two barefooted, blond-headed nephews, Aubrey and
Addison, shot out and sprinted toward me. Ten-year-old Aubrey
had a half gallon of ice cream under his arm and a spoon in the
opposing hand, and his younger brother was chasing him frantically with a spoon of his own. They were both laughing and completely ignored my request that they close the door behind them.

Aubrey brushed by me and raced in the direction of his house,
which was right next door. Addison stopped abruptly and stood
stock-still as something apparently caught his eye. Before I could
give him the bug lecture and ask that he please go back and close
the front door, Addison flung the spoon (which I assumed came

from my kitchen) into the bushes, dove headlong with arms out-
stretched, and pounced belly flop–style into the grass beside me.
Just as quickly he was back on his feet with filthy hands cupped.
"I got it," he said quietly.

"Wow. What is it?" I asked, and bent down closer to have a look.

Addison popped whatever he held into his mouth and stared
at me with blue eyes steeped in mischief. Sticking out his tongue,
he exposed a large grasshopper. The bug sprang from his mouth,
right into my hair. I let out a startled squeal and began swatting
my head to free the grasshopper from tangled entrapment. It
seemed this was the funniest stunt the seven-year-old had ever
managed. He was laughing so hard he could barely scamper
home. As he reached the woods between the two houses, I heard
a faint reminder from the older brother: "Don't forget to tell Linny
about the lamp."

"It was an accident" was the last thing I heard from the nephews
as I turned and started once again toward the house, wondering
what had been added to the ever-growing list of household fatali-
ties. The lawn, as shaggy as everything else in my life, needed
help. Maybe I should cut the grass before getting cleaned up, I
thought as I waded through the front yard to the mower. A dozen
or so yanks on the pull cord were ignored by the mower, and just
as I was resorting to checking the gas tank, the phone rang. Hoping it was my mother rescuing me with an invitation to dinner, I
dashed into the house and grabbed the phone before it completed
its third ring.

It wasn't Mom, but I was delighted to hear instead the voice of
a friend from my swordfishing days, Jim Budi, who was calling
from Fairhaven, Massachusetts. While Jim and I exchanged the

usual greetings, I stepped over the kids' life jackets, a BB gun, a slingshot, a pair of muddy sneakers, and a bottle of glue to make my way to the freezer door, which had been (not surprisingly) left wide open. By the time I'd wiped up a puddle of Elmer's glue from the floor, Jim was down to the business of his call. He was looking to hire a captain to run one of the four swordfishing long-liners he managed. I had had similar conversations with Jim over the past few years and had always thanked him for considering me. But the timing had never been right.

I looked around my disheveled living room. I glanced out the window. The yard was sorely in need of taming. The truck was on its last gasp. My lobster traps were not producing enough to pay expenses. There was a pile of unpaid bills on the kitchen table. The timing would never be right, I thought. Or maybe this was what the right timing looked like? Every year that passed and I put off my return to swordfishing, the prospect of ever getting back out on the water became more remote. "I can do it," I said, astounding myself with the level of irresponsibility I had achieved.

I felt myself flush with excitement. I was going swordfishing. I had never relaxed my grip on my most coveted identity—swordboat captain—and now I was going to live the dream one more time. I felt big and strong and courageous. I have always believed that the ability to answer the door when the right opportunity knocks is what separates truly successful people from the crowd. Here I am, I thought. My life is safe and comfortable. I have a deep yearning to go out of that comfort zone one more time. I need the reward that comes with great risk. I was truly living a blessed life. Cool things just kept happening to me (a few unpaid bills and an overgrown lawn notwithstanding). Jim Budi was offering me the chance to accept what might become my biggest personal challenge yet. And in classic "Casey at the Bat"–style, any truly great one would approach the plate one last time. I just hoped I was doing it with better results than Casey!

Before the end of our conversation, I understood that I would be reporting for duty in one week with a crew of four men. We were to make two trips to the Grand Banks of Newfoundland. The boat in the offing for me was the *Seahawk*, a boat I knew from the past as a solid producer and one that at just sixty-three feet in length was at the smaller end of the Grand Banks fleet. I tried not to focus on the fact that the most recent captain had died aboard her during a fishing trip.

The *Seahawk* had been dry-docked for several months following this unfortunate incident and was now for sale. Although a deal was in the making for her purchase, the prospective buyer hadn't actually come up with any cash. So, the owner of the boat was happy to have her recommissioned. Things had changed slightly during my sabbatical from swordfishing, Jim explained. But the changes were mostly just new rules and gear regulations that he could easily explain when I arrived in Fairhaven to help get the boat ready for sea. All I needed to do was hire four men who could pass the background check that the owner required and get the mandatory Protected Species Safe Handling, Release and Identification Workshop's vessel-operator certificate. This workshop was offered in Florida, Jim explained, and was designed to train fishermen how to safely handle and release protected species should they encounter any. In the case of long-lining sword off the Grand Banks, turtles were the concern. And although I had never killed a turtle, I realized the importance of getting the certificate.

No problem, I thought as I placed the phone back into the receiver. I'll fly to Florida, get certified, book my return flight into Boston, and beg or hire a ride to Fairhaven. All I needed to do was hire my crew. And tie up some loose ends here at home. "Loose" was an understatement. I had ends flopping around everywhere, at every turn. The prospect of the thrill of catching swordfish was all I needed to get very motivated to tidy up my life in short order. I would bring a load of traps ashore tomorrow. I would do whatever was required to jump on this opportunity of my lifetime. But for now I would concentrate on assembling a top-notch gang for this comeback trip.

My mind raced ahead of my Rolodex as I frantically searched the dog-eared cards for Ringo's number. Did I have it under "Tom"? Did I have it crammed in with the Cs, for "crew"? I couldn't imagine going offshore without Tom Ring. I had had the good fortune of great crew members while captaining the *Hannah Boden* and knew that Ringo would be my first-round draft pick for the upcoming trip. Like me, he hadn't been swordfishing in the last decade. But, also like me, he'd been working on the water and dreaming about a comeback and waiting for the right opportunity. And now opportunity was knocking.

Ringo answered the phone, but he wasn't about to answer the knock. He had been gillnetting with the same captain for some years now and wouldn't feel right about leaving him in the lurch, he said. I wondered when Ringo had become scrupulous. "Besides," he explained, "my life has changed. I'm a grandfather." That was a tough one to argue with. Ringo had played the grandfather card. There was no sense trying to sway him. Ringo was out. November would be a possibility, he said, as his captain liked to go hunting and would be taking time off to do so. Two trips beginning mid-September; I had no intention of hanging on through the dreaded month of November, which is historically the wickedest weather-wise. Besides, the opportunity was here, it was now. Like tide and time, it would not wait. Ringo would sit this one out.

So Ringo's life had changed. No shit—whose hadn't? If your life doesn't change in the course of a decade, there must surely be some moss growing. I had settled down significantly in the last ten years, and the changes had been good. Although I'd never married, I did have the best guyfriend, Simon. Sure, I had pushed for a permanent relationship, including a ring. But Simon just couldn't get there. We did, however, go dutch treat on a cement mixer. And that's about as committed as I'd ever been. I had long given up on the wedding bells. And furthermore, Ringo's grand-child, just for the record, is his wife's daughter's baby. Not even blood related! *His* life had changed. What about mine?

If Ringo could claim he was a grandfather, I could say I was a mother. In fact, talk about change and responsibility—I had be-come the legal guardian of a teenage girl just one year before. I'd gone from zero to fifteen with the stroke of a pen! Granted, I was still in the process of getting to know Sarai and hoping I would do a better job than her former guardian, who was currently await-ing trial on federal charges. But Sarai would be well cared for in my absence, I justified. In fact, the more I thought about it, the more comfortable I was about shirking this particular responsi-bility. The entire island community had stepped up to mother and mentor both Sarai and me in our new roles. I counted out the months on my fingers. She's a boarding student. It's now Septem-ber, and she doesn't have a break until Thanksgiving. I'd be home

by then. I would ask my sister to act as guardian while I was at
sea. And Simon . . . well, he was at his place in Vermont. He'd
hardly miss me. My parents would miss me, though. I paused to
consider that they were a lot younger when I'd last headed offshore, but they could still fend for themselves for two months. So
I needn't worry about them. They would be as nervous as they'd
always been when I was at sea but would understand that this
could very well be my last chance to go. Who knows, maybe my
folks' status would prohibit me from going in the future. I *had* to
go now! I could easily leave the lobstering. I'd bring my traps
ashore before taking off, and I'd ask a couple of friends to keep an
eye on my boat. I was supposed to begin writing the third book in
my mystery series. That could wait. Ringo couldn't drop everything and go offshore for two months? It'd drive him nuts knowing I was catching swordfish without him. He'd be sorry.

As I flipped through the cards, it soon became clear that most of
the guys I would like to have fishing with me could not pass muster
in any background check. One consequence of not keeping your
nose clean is that there are chances that you will not be eligible
for. These guys did not deserve this opportunity, I decided.

My second choice after Ringo would be Kenny Puddister, the
redheaded Newfy I had worked with for years. Kenny would probably be fishing with Scotty aboard the *Eagle Eye II*. It wouldn't be
very ethical of me to try to steal him. Besides, if I were Kenny and
had to choose between the two captains, me or Scotty, I would go
with Scotty, too. There was no point in putting myself through
that humiliation. I had absolutely no way of getting in touch with
choice number three, Carl. He owed me some money, so there

was little chance that he'd surface if I put feelers out. James was in Ireland. I hadn't heard from Ivan in years. I hesitated on a card on which I had written "moron." The moron would be available. But I just couldn't do it. I had signed on to spend sixty days a minimum of a thousand miles from home, bobbing around the North Atlantic Ocean during the height of hurricane season in pursuit of swordfish. I would be living and working in less-than-optimum conditions very closely with four men. In the past I had not minded working with men who behaved like animals—or morons, for that matter. They got the job done. I had always hired from the neck down. But at the age of forty-seven, I realized that I had changed and that perhaps my criteria for crew needed to change.

I took a break from the Rolodex to check e-mail and was happy to find a note from Jim Budi. Jim must have some innate sense about things, I marveled, as I read his e-mail. He had sent a list of potential crew members, with short bios and contact information. He listed five guys, all of whom had experience fishing on the boats he managed that constituted the "Eye Fleet" and all of whom he'd recently contacted regarding work. The names, except for one—Mike Machado—were unfamiliar to me.

The first bio read like a personal ad, with details about eye color and zodiac sign. No thanks, I'm all set on that front, I thought. The second sounded like a backwoods, Rambo type of guy. Nope. I've fished with the likes of them. Not this time. The third one Jim referred to as "the Silver Fox" and noted that he had "been sober for two weeks." Great, an old drunk. I'm not that desperate. I have a friend who trumps the Fox—out of rehab and straight for three months—but I'm not taking him offshore. Possibility number four was "Mr. Weeks." Would I have to call him "Mister"? Too weird for me. The additional comment that Mr. Weeks had actually captained the *Seahawk* for a short while and might need an occasional reminder that he was no longer in charge sealed his fate. One boat plus two captains equals nightmare. This was beginning to resemble audition week for *American Idol*. It's one thing to accept opportunity and quite another to capitalize on it. The right crew would be essential in maximizing this opportunity. So much for Jim's suggestions.

The next call had to be a yes. Who's a sure thing? *Surething*! The name of Dave Hiltz's boat was an omen. Why hadn't Hiltzie come to mind first? Dave Hiltz was a friend, a fellow islander, and a fisherman. He'd been after me to take him swordfishing since I'd known him. I'd promised him many times that if and when I had an opportunity to make a trip to the Grand Banks, I would take him along. Dave was the epitome of squeaky clean. Boat owners like that. I figured that he would be home from hauling lobster traps by now, as it was late afternoon and he always started his days at first light. Hiltzie would make a good shipmate and a great crew member. And if he ended up going, he could fill the position of the token greenhorn. Normally the green guy had little or no time at sea and often had no fishing experience whatsoever. Dave Hiltz was a lifelong fisherman. He worked his own boat, fishing for lobster, halibut, and scallops, and had fished with others for shrimp down south. Because he had never caught a sword, he was technically green. Dave Hiltz is a nice man and one of my best friends. Notorious for his temper and tall tales, Hiltzie would be a colorful addition, I mused, as I dialed his number.

Whether his decision was totally situational (the poorest

lobster season in his experience) or the fulfillment of a lifetime dream (Dave's grandfather had been a Grand Banks fisherman) mattered not. Dave Hiltz was on board with no question or hesitation and plenty of enthusiasm. It was a yes all the way. Then, minutes later, he called back with his wife, Debra, on the extension. The voice of reason wanted to know if Dave would make any money on this swordfishing voyage.

Ah, there it was, the dreaded money question. I said all the things that I had repeated so many times during my career. I promised nothing. I explained that we would be working on a share basis and that compensation would be commensurate with pounds of fish landed. Settlements were pretty standard, I explained. After the fish went to market, trip expenses—bait, fuel, grub, et cetera—were deducted from the gross, and the remainder would be split between the owner and the fishing crew and captain. While I was careful not to predict a gold rush, I was confident that I could still produce. Although I had not vocalized it, I knew that this could be one of the greatest comebacks in fishing history. Dave would be leaving his wife and their thirteen-year-old daughter, Abigail, for two months with no guarantee that he'd return with a cent—or that he'd return at all. I recall Debra making a comment about whaling, and I confessed that commercial fishing hadn't progressed far. Opportunity for a unique experience—for sure. Opportunity for financial gain—potentially.

The obvious risks inherent in commercial fishing—like those to life, limb, and livelihood—are concerns of mere mortals. Real fishermen risk other things that are less easily explained. In my present situation, the risks involved in returning to something I'd once felt so passionate about were many and not as tangible as fears for personal safety or pocketbook. I risked falling out of love with fishing itself. I'm good at catching fish. Is this why I like to do it? What if I were to suddenly realize that I did not enjoy the hunt? What if I were absolutely turned off by blood and guts? What if my heart didn't race with the tugging of a fish on the line? And, God forbid, what if I'd lost the ability to catch fish? My entire identity and self-definition were at stake. Disillusionment, should it occur, would hit hard. The half-full glass was not my style. Perhaps the same scenario could be seen as enlightenment. Either way I spun it, learning the truth was worth the risk, I concluded.

In spite of the financial risks, Debra seemed willing enough to let Dave go. And he seemed elated to be going. Escape? Maybe. I knew well the enticement of going to sea and forgetting about what is lying in wait back on solid land. The sea has an uncanny ability to swallow troubles (even if it spews up a few new ones to take their place). The problem is that your troubles are patient, and you do eventually have to come ashore. But at the moment, my troubles were few, and getting fewer, I realized as I dialed up my old fishing buddy Arthur Jost.

It was more of a courtesy call than an invitation to go fishing; I knew that Archie would be excited to hear the news of my upcoming adventure. He would be envious, for sure. But at sixty-six years old and somewhat overweight, Archie probably realized that his commercial-fishing days were now in the wake of his life. Besides, Archie always had so much going on with family and friends that he'd never be able to shake free. He owned and ran two businesses, selling hot tubs and fuel additives. Between marketing, selling, installing, servicing, and distributing his wares,

Arch found time to be in the midst of a major house-construction project in the Bahamas. He and his wife, Marge, had moved from Montauk, New York, to Stuart, Florida, several years before and had just begun to enjoy a semiretired status. I knew Arch as a chronic workaholic who would never fully retire. When I visited, I literally chased him from garage to shop to warehouse to truck to backhoe to boat and always marveled at his energy and expertise in all things. There was nothing Archie couldn't do. It was always fun to talk boats and fish with him, because he walked the walk. My primary goal in placing a call to Archie was to receive a huge "Go, girl!" I knew that I would be hearing a lot of things to the contrary once word got out.

Archie answered my call with a cheerful voice that always made me glad I had dialed his number. I couldn't contain my excitement and just started blurting things out. Because I had no intention of inviting him to go fishing with me, I was shocked when he interrupted and informed me that he was making the trip and would bring his friend Tim Palmer along, too. "This will be great! I always wanted to go to the Grand Banks with you. You'll need a good engineer. You know I can fix anything. Timmy is a real good guy. You'll love having him aboard. I'll start getting some stuff together. I'll need an address to ship things to. This will be great." I was hesitant to remind Arch that he was a grandfather. I remembered my conversation with Hiltzie's wife and fought the urge to ask Arch if I could speak with Marge. Marge would be more sensible, I reasoned.

As it turned out, Marge had no sense either. Twenty-four hours after the original call from Jim Budi, Archie had already shipped to the dock the first of several loads of engine-room supplies he wanted to be sure to have, and he and Tim had booked tickets to Boston. Archie was fully invested now, with his wife's consent. And the more I heard from Arch and Tim, the more I believed that this opportunity was of the golden kind.

Completing the crew would be Mike Machado, the one man I found acceptable from Jim Budi's list of recommendations. I'd met Machado in Puerto Rico years back. At that time he was working for Captain John Caldwell aboard the original *Eagle Eye*. John Caldwell had a reputation for running a tight ship as well as catching fish, so I assumed that Machado would be an ace. With a verbal voucher from Jim Budi on Machado's ability to clean fish, which was the hole in this crew in need of filling, I was satisfied that I had put together an all-star cast.

News of the upcoming trip spread and covered the island like blueberries in August. There was real electricity in the buzz— well-wishers had high hopes for our success and clung to the possibility of more island men getting similar opportunities in this very poor lobster year. I had the names and numbers of nearly every able body when I left the town dock and headed off with a "write when you find work" tone in the farewell. I recalled the apropos words of my friend, first captain, and fishing mentor Alden Leeman: "I want to make one more ripple before I'm done." My optimism was saying "splash."

The tingle of excited anticipation was not overshadowed by the old familiar burden of expectation. Greater risk always meant greater reward, I reminded myself as the last of the hand wavers disappeared in the wake of the mail boat that ferried Dave Hiltz and me away to the mainland, the first short leg of what promised to be a long voyage. Challenge was what had been missing in my life. I needed to be shocked, stunned, scared. I needed to react to emergency. I needed to fend off ever-looming disaster. I needed to fight the forces that converge at the center of the funnel. I needed to be daunted by a task bigger than getting a grasshopper out of my hair. I was aware that fulfilling these needs was an exercise in personal indulgence. And if I happened, in the course of meeting selfish goals, to succumb to the inherent physical danger, Sarai was my only real responsibility. She needed me. She didn't know it, but I did. Irresponsible? Selfish? Perhaps. But I needed to be offshore.

"personal growth"

CHAPTER 2

The Crew

The time had come to throw the lines off the dock. I wondered if the tightness in my gut was the same nervous excitement I'd experienced so many times on sailing day through the years. Or was this something altogether different? I would know soon enough, I told myself as I put the engine in gear to spring the *Seahawk* away from the pier. The stern eased out to form a wedge of space between the rail of the boat and the dock. Satisfied that I could now slip away without even the faintest caress of pilings, I yelled down to Dave Hiltz to release the spring line, totally severing our last tie to solid land, like the cutting of an umbilical cord. I was full of the apprehension of independence and exhilarated by anticipation of the same. I had been wondering how this would feel. Now I knew.

Let's face it: There had to be some blowback from ten years of

fellow islander

additional age and absence from the swordfishing industry that I had loved for so long and spent the last decade openly and vocally missing. I was struck by a new notion: that my proudly professed love affair with long-lining Grand Banks–style might have been a defense mechanism, love feigned in denial of the possibility that I had wasted nineteen precious years of my life chasing fish in faraway waters. This hazardous image crossed my mind as I nodded to Archie to loosen the stern line. FAT

Archie, Tim, and Machado—who had been a no-show up until minutes before loosening lines—filled the work deck. The backs of these three XXXLs were impressive. "Ohio State," they had already dubbed themselves, in reference to their combined weight totaling an entire offensive football line. Dave Hiltz joined them in facing the stern to wave last good-byes. At six feet tall and two hundred pounds, he looked like a shrimp. Dave's dark goatee added a slightly sinister air to what otherwise looked like it would be a fun-loving and good-natured group.

TIM. 36

Tim was the first to give up on the stern and turn forward. His body was nothing short of awesome. Like a man and a half, Tim Palmer looked like a machine—square, mechanical, and built to work. His boyish face and grin, framed in Dennis the Menace–style brown hair, contradicted what stood from his chin down, in the best Photoshopped fashion. Freckles trickled across the bridge of his nose connecting tanned cheeks. At thirty-six, Tim was the baby of our new seagoing family.

If Tim was our newborn, then Archie was definitely the patriarch. Not that Arch was ancient, but sixty-six is relatively old for crewing aboard a Grand Banks trip even if you don't look your age. I suspected that Arch's blond hair may have had some chemical

ARCHIE 66

help in staying blond, but the brightness in his blue eyes was all natural. He had already become the caregiver of our group, counseling, lecturing when needed, and handing out Band-Aids. Because of his age, I had planned for Arch to have a role of light duty regarding deck work and to have him take responsibility for the cooking and extra night watches when we reached the fishing grounds so that the rest of us could get a bit more sleep. He turned and began coiling a dock line, then flashed a huge smile up toward the wheelhouse. Archie was truly thrilled to be part of this team. And I knew he would be a real asset. He's just one of those smart guys who you suspect retained all of his incidental education while having no interest in formal schooling. Any apprehension I had about Archie's age was quickly overshadowed by his ability and attitude. Age, like gender, is only a problem if it's allowed to be.

To say that Machado rounded out the crew would be an unfortunate pun. He had put on about eighty pounds in the twenty years since I'd first met him and was now quite hefty. Salt-and-pepper hair and a jovial face made everyone like Machado at first sight, which was fortunate, seeing as until his last-minute appearance he was becoming increasingly disliked by his shipmates. His South Boston talk was tough, but his words were gentle. He was, I decided in five minutes, the funniest man I'd ever met. A natural comedian, Machado reminded me of Jackie Gleason. Genuinely satisfied that he was the man for the fish-butchering job, as we pulled away from the dock I was able to forgive his tardiness and the fact that he'd skipped the preceding week of backbreaking and filthy work we'd had to conduct without him. Levity thrown in at the right juncture to help in a heavy situation can be as valuable as light-footedness.

funny

MACHADO

I cast a glance in the opposite direction from where the last dock line had come. Somewhat forlorn-looking, Simon gave me a shy, crooked smile and half a wave. I thought I sensed a shaking of his head, as if he were wondering what I could possibly have been thinking when I agreed to take the *Seahawk* offshore for two months. I shrugged my shoulders and mouthed, "I know." The only slight opposition I'd received with my announcement of returning to this world had been from Simon. He had asked what I was trying to prove. Although I'd answered, "Nothing," the question haunted me a bit. When I first began fishing at the age of nineteen, I was told that all I needed was a strong back and a weak mind. That proved to be true for many years. Now, at the age of forty-seven, I have a stronger mind and a weaker back. Was this the question I needed to answer?

I'd been here before, feeling bad about leaving someone special on the dock. But I would never turn back, as I knew from experience that the misgivings and doubts would be promptly upstaged by the nerve-soothing activity of work that had become second nature. Once I had broken the visual connection with Simon, my eyes, my thoughts, and my energy were all focused ahead and into the future. Five hundred miles, sixty days, tons of fish . . . There are many ways to mark time at sea. And it was all ahead of us. There was nothing to look back at. This is what I do, I thought as I steered the *Seahawk* through the narrow slot in the hurricane barrier that embraced the port exit shared by Fairhaven and New Bedford, Massachusetts. And this was the easy part. The week leading up to our departure had been pure hell. To be free from the dock and what it represents is liberating.

Shortly after the call from Jim Budi, I had flown to Florida to

attend the "turtle release" workshop and returned to Boston's
Logan Airport fully certified and raring to go. Three of my four
crew members—Archie, Dave, and Tim—met me in Beantown
with a rental car. It was late at night, and everyone was tired. The
guys had spent the better part of the past week working long hours
aboard the *Seahawk* and seemed happy and relieved that their
captain had come to join them in preparing our boat for sea.

The one-hour ride to Fairhaven was filled with fast talk from
all three trying to bring me up to speed regarding the condition in
which they'd found the boat, the work (mostly dirty) they had
performed, and what needed to be done before we set sail. The list
of needs was indeed lengthy. But I was confident that this team
could burn through it beginning first thing the next morning. For
now, I thought, sleep was critical. I knew that the four of us had
two adjoining rooms to share at the local hotel, but before we
turned in for the night, the guys thought it necessary to show me
the boat. "We want to make sure you can't sleep either," said Tim
as we climbed out of the car at the dock. They all laughed. I knew
that nothing could be bad enough to rob me of this night's sleep.

The tide was at the right level for me to make an easy step
from pier to deck through the fish door, a square opening cut in
the hull through which swordfish are dragged from the water.
The first thing I noticed was that the boat was port-rigged—set
up to haul the fishing gear aboard on the left-hand side. This would
be a tiny obstacle, as I had always worked boats that were rigged
on the starboard side. Not much in the way of ambidextrous, I
realized that the time since my last haulback would work to my
advantage, as I was certainly out of practice hauling from the right
side. The next thing I noticed was that the *Seahawk* was much

smaller than I had remembered her being and that the work deck was cluttered with stuff that could only be described as junk.

"What's all this . . . shit?" I asked.

"That's stuff we took out of the forepeak when we cleaned. There wasn't any more room in the dumpster," Arch said, pointing to the steel garbage receptacle on the dock that was overflowing and surrounded by boxes and plastic buckets also stuffed with unrecognizable refuse that I assumed had all originated from the bowels of my new craft. "Those are the tools that I found worth trying to salvage," he said as he nodded in the direction of a large table made of a sheet of plywood and two sawhorses. The table was covered with a variety of rusted tools, including an assortment of adjustable wrenches that really belonged in the dumpster. "That's the best of it." I couldn't imagine what had filled the dumpster if these tools looked better in comparison.

Not far from the dumpster stood one dozen of the crummiest-looking beeper buoys I had ever seen. These electronic buoys are imperative to successful fishing. You attach them to the line as it is set into the water, and they assist in locating the gear once it is cut free from the boat and allowed to drift with the current. Steel canisters house batteries and electronic boards that act as sending units of specific frequencies received by the boat's radio direction finder. Each canister is ringed with flotation and topped with a two-piece, ten-foot antenna. Or at least that was how I remembered them. But not these. This dilapidated bunch of crap couldn't possibly belong aboard my boat, I hoped. Archie must have read my thoughts. "The electronics guy is coming in the morning to fix the beepers. None of them work."

And so it went for the entire eye-opening tour. Every compartment of the boat displayed signs of neglect. There seemed to be a total absence of anything decent to work with. All of the equipment, gear, and systems necessary for fishing far from shore for long periods of time were sorely lacking. There was a fresh coat of paint in the engine room and a rumor that the main engine had just been rebuilt. But other than that, things were shaky. There were three antique computers in the wheelhouse, but my tour guide confirmed optimistically that some local computer genius would perform miracles before we sailed.

The fo'c'sle (forecastle, or area beneath the forward part of the deck) was okay, except for the head, which sported a leaky plastic toilet that could have been ripped out of a decrepit camper, and the galley, which had been totally scavenged of utensils needed for eating or cooking. The bunks were adequate, except in number. One of us would have to sleep at the galley table. The bench seat on the starboard side had been extended, making it clear which side of the table was meant to be someone's bedroom. The extension had been covered with a cushiony pad. Nice touch, I thought as I sat and held my head in my hands. The first of the usual series of second thoughts crept in. "Wait till you see the lazarette. It's a nightmare," Tim said in reference to the aftermost below-deck compartment that housed the steering gear and rudder shaft.

"Not tonight, man. I've seen enough. Let's get some rest and start fresh tomorrow," I said. There was nothing the men could show me that would persuade a change of heart in me, I tried to convince myself. The boat was rough. I had fished worse. I liked challenge, didn't I?

"How about checking out the *Eagle Eye II*," suggested Hiltzie. "She's beautiful! I sure wish we were going fishing with that boat.

Wanna see? She'll make you feel a lot worse." The *Eagle Eye II*, one of the other boats that would be competing with us for the catch, was tied to the dock directly behind us. At close to a hundred feet in length, she dwarfed the sixty-three-foot *Seahawk*. No doubt she was younger and more beautiful. But jumping ship was not an option.

"I don't want to feel worse. Let's go check in." The men reluctantly agreed, and off we went to the "dormitory," where we left the door open between the two rooms and talked and laughed about the predicament that I'd gotten the group into, until finally drifting off to a very short sleep. I wondered whether the boat was as bad as I perceived or if perhaps I'd been spoiled by captaining the *Hannah Boden* most recently, which in comparison was a yacht. I remembered my years fishing the *Gloria Dawn*. Now, that boat was a wreck. I was young and proud to be captain of her. My greatest accomplishment during my four-year reign of the *Gloria Dawn* had been returning to the dock each trip. Even the owner looked surprised to see my crew throwing lines. I wondered whether I would feel the same pride running the *Seahawk* or if that, like youth, had passed.

The men and I spent a full week working from sunup to dark and laughing ourselves to sleep in the dormitory. Jim Budi worked along with us and managed a small army of professionals who patched, condemned, and replaced everything that time and budget allowed before the well was declared dry and the hourglass empty. Our time had come. It was my last chance to back out.

Captain Scott Drabinowicz had arrived at the *Eagle Eye II* in time to throw grub and bait aboard, and he was ready to go. Scotty hadn't changed a bit, I thought. The only exception was the addition of a ponytail. He was a big, blond juggernaut of a fisherman who'd been very successful. I remembered that Scotty had always been extremely scientific in his approach to catching swordfish. He had freely shared information and lent good insight. I had always enjoyed fishing around him in the past and was looking forward to doing it again. He was certainly the right guy to hold my hand as I reentered blue-water fishing. Although we had a friendly competition between us—a buck to the catcher of the single biggest fish— I truly believed that Scotty wished me success. Steaming and fishing in his company gave me peace of mind. His boat was the mother ship of the small fleet, and Scotty was like the godfather of sword. Just seeing him was enough to bolster my resolve and check any misgivings. I just couldn't falter with Scotty as a witness.

We had certainly transformed the *Seahawk*, I thought proudly as Archie lowered the outriggers while I steered toward the Cape Cod Canal. I was plenty nervous about the age and condition of nearly every system on the boat. But I would keep those reservations to myself. We could have spent another month working at the dock, but here we were, heading to sea. Arch stuck his head into the wheelhouse. I smiled and pushed a thumb into the air. "We did it. We got her ready for fishing."

"I'm a little worried about leaving port without everything working," my friend confided. "The weather fax and computer software for weather information weren't fixed. You don't have any fish-finding technology working. All you have is the surface-temperature gauge and a barometer. And the glass is broken on the barometer."

"Yeah, it'll be like old times." I feigned excitement and optimism. "The old gal may look a bit rough. But she's stable and capable."

Although I was referring to the boat, I couldn't help but think the same could be said of her captain. Jeez, I thought, maybe I should spend a little less time inventorying the ship and start taking stock of myself. Maybe the *Seahawk* wasn't the weak link. Age and lack of use were certainly liabilities in terms of the boat's anticipated performance. Boats do not get better with age. In fact, immediately following the maiden voyage, a vessel begins a steady and stunningly quick-paced decline. But what about me? It was too late to abandon ship with a Mayday from second thoughts. And there was plenty of time for bailing out the swelling self-doubt.

I had left the dock in the most exhausted state I'd ever felt and was embarking on an endurance test. My legs were already weary of standing at the wheel when I exited the canal into Cape Cod Bay, and I shuddered at the numbers on the GPS that indicated 144 hours to go to reach our destination, a vague spot east of the Grand Banks that I had programmed in to get us headed in a general direction. I would only grow more tired as the trip wore on. What was more tired than dead exhaustion? Now that we had left landmass far enough behind to take a chance, I flipped on the automatic pilot and prayed that it would function well enough to allow me to sit down. It did. I briefly recalled a severe ocean storm that had kept me on my feet and fighting the wheel for forty-eight hours straight. I hoped that I would have some time to get into shape before Mother Nature scheduled any marathons.

I sat and mentally measured my tolerance and ability to endure what I knew the next sixty days had in store for me. Out of necessity, I had, early in my career, developed my own techniques for the heavy, physical-strength part of swordfishing. I had developed female ways of putting moves on what most people would consider man's work. Today I was not only female but I was also on the waning side of middle age. A lot changes in a woman's body between the ages of thirty-seven and forty-seven. Lack of real, tough work had resulted in a fifteen-pound weight loss—and all muscle at that. So I was now smaller and not as physically strong. I would certainly have to develop all new techniques to do what the job required. I would have to, as my old boss Alden had advised in answer to any complaint I registered over eight years of working for him, "toughen up."

As the sun went down and we steamed into the Gulf of Maine, I contemplated my own seaworthiness. The ocean's expectations and demands are so high that anyone who goes upon it must be worthy on many levels. I wondered how I would respond to the sleep deprivation that would surely begin when the first hooks were baited and set. I had always been able to function on four hours a night. Adrenaline had been my caffeine. Would adrenaline flow at the rate it had ten years earlier? Or had that dried up? I could, I reasoned, compensate with coffee. What about my hands? I inspected knuckles that were just beginning to show signs of arthritis. I would need to grab and pull a minimum of twelve hundred snaps from the main line every day we fished. And the snaps were made of the heaviest-gauge wire—gorilla snaps, we called them. I hoped that Archie had brought a bushel of ibuprofen. I wondered how my legs and back would stand up to pulling leaders tight with huge fish that resisted being caught. I had loved every strain generated by hundred-fish days a decade before. Perhaps I would need to stretch and warm up with a few calisthenics each morning. Good thing I had such a mighty crew. Would I have the balance and strength to keep my feet under me in heavy weather? My legs weren't as strong as they could be. I should have kept myself in better shape. What if my legs buckled every time a giant green wave broke over the top of me? That could be dangerous. Jesus, even my eyes were shot, I realized as I donned my magnifiers to check the navigational chart. I'd never needed those before. No, I thought, age would not be an asset in the physical realm.

I found a notebook and pen and made out a watch bill that listed the guys in order of the watches they would soon begin. Ten years earlier I would have started the first watch myself at 10:00 P.M. Tonight I wouldn't make it to 8:30. Maturity can't hold a candle to youthfulness. Unless, I considered, it's a mental/emotional thing. This endurance test would certainly go beyond physical. Mentally I needed to be stronger and wiser. Decisions were once based on gut reaction. I'd often made the right decision for the wrong reason. I'd done things purely from the strength of knowing that I could. Now maybe I would be more thoughtful with the realization of the possibility that perhaps I could not. I hoped that the past ten years had taught me something. I must be smarter now than I was when I'd last captained a swordboat. But what about quickness of mind? Would I react to emergencies fast enough? I had always prided myself on my mental reflexes in the face of danger or disaster. I had always been confident beyond reason. Maybe it was healthier to be wiser, more mature, and less confident.

Then I wondered how old was *too* old. Although I couldn't put my finger on it, I knew that I had gained something in seaworthiness that was more important than sea legs. The surest, most telling, indisputable sign of my age was the thought process I was

reaction vs reason   youth vs age
confidence vs doubt

now going through. I had never before wondered about nor doubted myself after the lines were cast and the boat was at sea.

Hell, I'm not that old, I scoffed, snapping myself out of this reverie of neurosis. I mean, I still had my own teeth and everything, and was thankful for every one of them as Arch appeared with a plate of food for my dinner. He stayed and chatted and watched me eat for a few minutes. "Isn't this great?" he asked. "Isn't this a beautiful night?" I felt foolish for the time I'd wasted dwelling on my age. Here was a man old enough to be my father, happy as could be and thankful to be here. Arch wasn't doubting his ability. I hadn't even noticed the sunset.

"Everything's good in the engine room. Timmy has that under control. This boat is really comfortable. I'll bet she's a great sea boat," Arch said as he squinted out the back window at the last of the colorful sky. I dove into the steak and Stove Top stuffing like it was the last meal I would see. It was all smothered in gravy. Nothing could have been more unhealthy and fattening. I never would have worried about *that* ten years ago either. But I didn't complain, because I had appointed Archie to do the cooking. We hadn't had to draw straws to see who was stuck with the chore of feeding the group. "I feel good. This feels right. You feel good?" Archie asked.

"Yes. This is great, Arch. I feel great," I lied.

CHAPTER 3

Outward Bound

Ripe and one sliver shy of full, the cantaloupe moon shone a flashlight beam along our path as we steamed east through the Gulf of Maine. It was glassy calm, and running lights glowed dimly on the stabilizing birds at the ends of the booms, rounding their edges to appear like jet engines under wings, red on port and green on starboard. This breathless night allowed us to haul the birds out of the water and gain a full knot in speed, as they normally ride below the surface to retard the roll of the boat and they slow us down in the process. The steady drone of the diesel two decks below added a soothing hum to the slow, gentle rocking of mysterious origin. The last of the lime green landmass had crept from the edge of the radar screen as the faded umbrella of city lights closed over our wake. At sea—it's more a feeling than it is a place.

It was this feeling, the state of being at sea, that I hadn't experienced in ten years. This sensation is the result of living the total contradiction of burden and freedom. I am the captain, I thought. The freedom to make all decisions, unquestioned and without input, was something that I had missed during my sabbatical. To be held ultimately, although not solely, responsible for the lives and livelihoods of a loyal and capable crew was strangely exhilarating and empowering. But high hopes and expectations were weighty loads. It's the willingness, and not the ability, to bear that burden that separates captains from their crew. Right here and right now, as the *Seahawk* plodded along, I was fondly embracing the burden of that responsibility. Just being on the boat made me feel good. I was confident. And confidence is a key to success.

I tweaked a knob on the autopilot to correct our course two degrees and remain on a perfect heading according to the numbers displayed on both GPS's. As I eased myself back into the captain's chair, Arch pulled himself up the narrow stairway and into the dark-paneled wheelhouse beside me. "Everything is secure below. Timmy is in the engine room doing a few things, Dave is reading a magazine at the galley table, and Machado is sleeping," he reported. "I really like Machado. He's so funny! I think he'll more than make up for not being around to help at the dock. You got a great crew!"

"Thanks, Arch. I know I do." I meant it. Confidence in my crew fed my personal confidence. I believed that this was the best crew I had ever sailed with. Certainly the most mature; we probably wouldn't be plagued by the usual crew problems that stem from basic personality differences and lack of sleep. I wouldn't have to break up any fistfights or garnish any wages as punishment for poor behavior. Small squabbles could be annoying, I knew. And nothing was more exasperating than trying to reason with real, solid, mutual hatred when both parties are virtually connected at the hip for an extended voyage. Liking one another was huge. As far as work ethics go, nothing beats the older, more experienced guys. It's very much like the "young bull/old bull" thing. Four of the five of us owned and operated our own boats, so we already knew the basic moves that otherwise needed to be taught. Mike Machado was the only non-captain aboard, but he was also the only one other than me with any Grand Banks fishing experience. And between the two of us, I suspected that we had racked up more miles along the salty way than any pair I could think of. "Yes," I said, "I think we have a winning team aboard. Just the right combination of talents and strengths."

"Speaking of talents and strengths, here I am," Tim said laughingly as he popped his head through the back door of the wheelhouse behind Archie. "The engine room is looking good. The water maker is cranking out, and the ice machine is making great ice—lots of it. I just shoveled. How's the list?" he asked, referring to whether or not the boat was leaning. I looked directly at the bow to determine that we were indeed not listing to either side and gave a silent nod. I was happy to forgo the usual lecture on the importance of keeping the boat on an even keel and the dangers inherent in not doing so, which is why I'd asked Tim to compensate by moving ice or fuel.

"Why didn't you tell me? I would have helped you shovel," said Archie.

"You take care of the galley, and the rest of us will handle the shoveling. Thanks for dinner, by the way. It was great," Tim said. I was relieved that Timmy had understood without having to be told that Archie was valuable in many ways and that none of his assets were in evidence on the end of a shovel. At his age and with the range of experience and breadth of knowledge that Archie had concerning just about anything, I didn't want to waste him in the fish hold. Again, I was appreciating the maturity level of my shipmates. I knew that Archie and Tim had a mutual liking and respect for each other, reminding me of father and son.

"I'm gonna call Marge tomorrow and get a recipe for chicken," Arch said. "Do you mind if I hook up the satellite phone in this corner? It's the only place the antenna wire reaches. Everyone can use it to make calls." He was twisting the small coupling at the end of the rubber-coated wire that came through a hole in the aft bulkhead and terminated in the corner he'd mentioned. The five of us had a lot in common, I realized. Our similarities went beyond the fishing gene. Food was of utmost importance, as was family. So a call home for a chicken recipe was a no-brainer. "I'm gonna fix that computer on my watch tonight. Did you find the manual for the weather fax? I know I can get that going. I bungeed the hell out of our stateroom. These things are coming in really handy so far," he said as he pulled a short loop of bungee cord out of a hip pocket. "These and the two-part epoxy . . . I can keep us going with this stuff." I had always known Archie as a guy with a short attention span. I guess you'd call it adult ADD.

"All I want to do is catch fish!" Hiltz had entered from the stairs and delivered what had already become his mantra. "Are we there yet, Skip?"

"Almost," I said, taking a closer look at our ETA below the track plotted on the only functioning computer monitor. "One thousand miles at seven point three knots—you can do the math," I told him as I slid out of the chair and leaned over the navigational chart built in on the after bulkhead. I've always preferred paper to electronics. I circled our present position in pencil and inscribed it with date and time.

"Where's Scotty?" That was Dave's other obsession. All he wanted to do was catch fish and know where Scotty was at all times. I understood his interest in the whereabouts of the *Eagle Eye II* as we went farther from shore than Dave had ever been—a lot farther—as a way to seek peace of mind through safety in numbers. As long as Scotty was in our vicinity, however wide or vague that might be, Dave seemed to relax.

I was more interested in the whereabouts of the *Bigeye*. Her captain, Chris Hanson—or "Chompers," as he's commonly known—is reputed to be one of the more disliked fishermen on the eastern seaboard. Although I had never encountered him, I had heard that Chompers had a history of doing whatever he had to do, regardless of fishing etiquette or safety, to pay his bills. From the radio chatter I gathered that the *Bigeye*'s captain was in Newfoundland outfitting for his Grand Banks debut.

I explained to Dave that Scotty couldn't be very far ahead of us, as I had caught a glimpse of the boat before the sun went down. We would be tracking slightly south of Scotty's course, since he had to steam to Newfoundland to pick up two crew members. His extra miles would gobble up what Scotty would otherwise have gained in a tiny speed advantage, so we would reach the grounds and make our first sets on the same evening. I suspected that the *Eagle Eye II* was capable of making better speed, but the price of fuel had bolstered her captain's innate patience, and he had pulled the throttle back. Satisfied that Scotty would not be out of radio range for the next sixty days, Dave eased into a story about the scars that ran the length of his arm, acquired while tub-trawling for halibut.

The four of us started trying to beat one another with tales of personal injuries inflicted at and by the sea. I joined in after Dave's second round, which ended in an episode of near amputation, and regaled the men with a litany of broken bones suffered, including a badly fractured ankle that snapped when I was suddenly buried in a pile of oversize offshore lobster traps. My crew literally dug me out of the mountain of gear that had given in to one hellacious wave, surprised to find me alive. I hobbled around on the ankle to finish the trip—two weeks—until it had healed out of kilter and had to be rebroken in a surgical procedure. Tonight, before the end of the third round, I had totally extolled my own bravery and pain threshold with the telling of my left hand's battle with a half hitch of thousand-pound-test monofilament. Although my hand won by parting the fishing line before being torn from my wrist, it was so badly swollen that it could not be put in a cast. So I did what any self-respecting fisherman would do and went back to sea with an Ace bandage and a bottle of aspirin. None of the episodes we chose to share proved much in the way of possessing brain cells. When the tales wound down to nicks and cuts and scars "that used to be right there," I decided to begin the night watches.

Arch was to stand watch first for two hours, waking Dave to do his two-hour stint. Tim was on the list at number three, and Machado was last and would wake me at 4:30 A.M. The watches would rotate, last man first up the next night, so that no one would be permanently saddled with the dreaded middle watches. Although the British navy would bristle at it, I had always referred to these as the "dog watches." We didn't sound bells every thirty minutes either. Night watches aboard a commercial fishing vessel require . . . well, watching. The men would watch the radar for traffic or other obstructions; the horizon for lights indicating traffic; the engine room for leaks, fires, and other problems; the ice machine for production; the GPS for our progress toward the fishing grounds; and the compass as a check on navigational electronics. Basically, the watch standers were responsible for keeping the boat on course and safe while the captain got some sleep.

I had many nightmarish stories of bad watch-standing practices to share. I spared my crew all the minute details, but the gist of the bedtime story I now chose to tell them was not aimed at putting them to sleep. There were many episodes of falling asleep and narrowly missing a fatal collision with another vessel or a landmass, but what appalled me even more were times when the watch stander was wide awake and making decisions in the well-intentioned interest of allowing the captain more sleep. In one case the man in charge had a bout of "get-home-itis." He looked at the chart and decided that a straight line was indeed the shortest distance between our present position and the dock that he so yearned to step onto. He changed course to shorten our steam, saving fuel, and manipulated our ETA to better suit the making of happy hour at the local watering hole. To this day I don't know how we made it through the dangerous shoals that his new course took us over. When I looked at our track line on the plotter that evening, I knew I'd seen a miracle. With the weather and sea conditions as they were, we should have been dead—all five of us.

I usually told a new crew about the time that a man fell asleep on watch and nearly ran us between a tug and its tow. And how I slapped him across the face to wake him. And how I fired him on the spot. But I didn't feel that was necessary tonight. Relying on luck to keep us alive did little to instill confidence. Relying on ability did. All of my men were savvy navigators and conscientious guys in general. So I should have no trouble sleeping away my eight-hour time off the wheel.

"Sleep tight, Linny," Arch said softly as I relinquished the chair to him. I wasn't accustomed to crew members calling me by such a familiar nickname. But Arch was an old and trusted friend who was more like family. And I preferred this nickname to "Ma," which is what Ringo and company had teasingly (and I chose to believe lovingly) called me. "We've got a lot to be proud of," Arch said as he took the chair. I knew that he was speaking to us as a group, so I hung around to acknowledge him. "This old girl is gonna be fine," he said as he patted the arm of the chair affectionately. "We brought her back to life from close to the grave. Think of what we've accomplished. And we haven't even caught a fish yet." Archie's voice cracked a bit. I sensed that he was very emotional, so I said good night. We were way beyond captain and crew aboard the *Seahawk*. We were a group of friends. It was cool.

"Thanks for bringing me fishing with you, Linny," said Hiltzie.

"You're welcome. Thank you for agreeing to make the trip." I hurried down the stairs into the stateroom I was to share with Archie and climbed into the top bunk. I'd never had a roommate on a fishing trip before and would have preferred my own space. But as long as I had to share, I was sure glad that it was with Archie. I hoped that Dave would still be thanking me at the end of the trip. This should really be a great experience for him, I thought as I pulled my sleeping bag up under my chin. And I was certainly feeling good about affording Dave this unique opportunity. If we could "hatch" the boat (fill the hold with fish) twice and hit the market at the right times, we'd all be happy about more than just a good experience. I wouldn't miss lobstering at all. I knew that Hiltzie wouldn't either.

I really despise sleeping bags. They make me feel all cooped up, like a bug in a cocoon, but not remotely cozy. I would have un-zipped the bag, freeing my claustrophobic feet from the skinny, dead end if I could have sat up. This had to be the smallest bunk I'd ever been crammed into. There wasn't an inch of extra room in it—even turning over would be prohibited by hips and shoul-ders. Good thing I could sleep on my back. Well, I couldn't expect to return to swordfishing after being away so long and step right aboard the best boat. Archie was right—the *Seahawk* was fine. Besides, it had taken me many years to work my way up to the *Hannah Boden*. And the *Seahawk* had plenty of character. Small bunks but big personality. Plus, there really weren't many boats left in the industry to choose from, even if I'd been given the option of running another, I realized as I started a mental count.

The position of skipper aboard a U.S. Grand Banks longline vessel is the absolute pinnacle of the commercial fishing world. I had always felt I was one of the few who remained of a dying breed of blue-water fishermen. And now that the number of Grand Bankers that sailed from the United States to catch sword-fish was down to half a dozen boats or so, being one of their cap-tains really placed me on an endangered-species list. I had always

taken great pride in introducing myself as a commercial fisherman, in spite of the public's misconceptions. We had long gotten
a bad (and sometimes deservedly so) rap for pillaging our way
through precious natural resources and promoting the eating of
unhealthy fish, but the tide had turned. The latest government
research had proved that the North Atlantic swordfish stock was
totally rebuilt. And my understanding was that science was saying the presence of selenium negated any adverse effect or danger
of mercury from consuming swordfish. I was proud to be heading
out in more of a politically correct and environmentally healthy
atmosphere than the one I had left. Yes, there is a certain snob
appeal in being a member of such an elite group of men who risk
all in pursuit of fish. And I had always felt that commercial fishing is a noble profession. We feed the world. But I had better get
to sleep soon, I told myself. There wasn't a lot of room in this
bunk for a swollen head.

Apparently all my happy thoughts produced great sleep. "Time
to get up, Skipper. Six o'clock," Machado said, loudly enough to
wake me but softly enough to not bother Archie, who was snoring in the bunk below. Had I really passed out for nine and a half
hours? The stretch down from my bunk was a long one for short
legs, and I had to place my foot carefully on the edge of the lower
bunk to avoid stepping on my roommate. I hustled into my boots
and scurried to the wheelhouse. "Good morning, Linda." Machado
greeted me with a huge infectious smile. "There's fresh coffee on
in the galley. Want a cup?"

"Thanks. I'll help myself in a few minutes. And thanks for the
extra rack time." I looked at the electronics and was pleased with
our progress and delighted that the crew had indeed kept us on

course through the night. Archie had somehow managed to get the second computer of three up and running. So now I had a backup. I was glad that Arch had tackled the computer, as I had almost no ability and even less patience. None of the multiple fish-finding software or weather-forecasting programs I'd been promised by Jim Budi worked, but the feed from the GPS seemed to function. So I had another fine track plotter that was driven by a system with which I was just becoming familiar, Nobeltec.

The rising sun in the windows made me squint, but I could never bring myself to wear sunglasses. There is something special about steaming directly into the sun and losing clear perception in its blaze on the ocean.

I thought about the Grand Banks and how aptly named the area is. Grand indeed; these fishing grounds have quite an imposing legacy. Two of the most renowned maritime catastrophes in history occurred there—the *Titanic* and the *Andrea Gail*—creating an aura to match that of the Bermuda Triangle among seamen who work or traverse the massive banks and the surrounding expanse deemed so grand. But it's not all about disaster. Not only do the Grand Banks produce some of the god-awfulest weather for mariners to contend with, but they also house some of the greatest fishing on the planet. Lifelong commercial fishermen who have never fished the Grand Banks are somewhat incomplete in their experience. To quote a late friend, "If you ain't been to the Grand Banks, you ain't been there." In my own career the Grand Banks is where I have fished among icebergs and killer whales. Now I felt the heat of the sun through the window on my face and chest and knew that soon I would be shivering and that this warmth would be a memory.

Mid-September is not the optimum time to begin the Grand Banks season. Swordfish fall into the category of "highly migratory," and typically they split from the Grand Banks when the Gulf Stream begins to pull offshore. This happens quickly and without notice, usually by the end of October. So we didn't have the luxury of time. And the moon had been full two nights before. Again, not optimum. I wished that we had reached the fishing grounds a week earlier, rather than having five days yet to go. Trips should ideally be in sync with the lunar cycle—steaming and dock time were best done when things were on the dark side and in the new-moon phase. I had always been most successful from the first quarter of the moon through the full and up to the last quarter. We were 100 percent off of my desired schedule. But the weather was beautiful. And that counts for a lot when you are getting your sea legs aboard a boat that is unknown to you. Besides, I recalled that Scotty, John Caldwell, and Jim Budi had all confirmed that fishing had recently been good off-moon. So, they said, don't worry about it. Ignore it, don't fret . . . I couldn't recall receiving such casual advice upon departing for a fishing trip in the past. I felt more relaxed and confident than I ever had in my years of captaining, and I attributed that to my age.

Far from worrying, I didn't have a care in the world as the *Seahawk* glided effortlessly along, bobbing slightly as if nodding her head or tapping a foot to some unheard music. This many hours into our steam and with the boat purring contentedly, my confidence level in the *Seahawk* was growing. I wandered around the boat and found Archie in the galley cooking oatmeal. He sang while he stirred. The other guys were in the three-sided steel structure on the stern called the setting house, where they were working on gear. There was a satisfaction about their work, I thought. These guys seemed genuinely happy to be here. And now they took pleasure in doing something that had a direct correlation to catching fish. All the sweaty, dirty chores we did at the dock served no purpose other than getting the boat offshore. Of course, getting off the dock is necessary, but making gear is more pertinent to what we all had a passion for—catching fish. In the past I had to get on the crew a bit to be meticulous about how the gear went together, as they often hurried through the job and the results could be sloppy. With Timmy's sportfishing experience, I knew that he would be anal about the gear—to a greater degree than even I was. As the greenhorn, Hiltzie would follow the lead set by the others. Dave Hiltz was bent on doing a good job, which was refreshing.

Machado measured four-hundred-pound-test monofilament fishing line in two-fathom lengths and crimped a snap—a small clothespin-type gadget that functions to secure leaders to the main line—onto one end. Over and over he made the "tops" of leaders while Tim cut "tails"—three-fathom pieces of the same mono onto which he attached hooks using crimps. In this case they were D crimps, sized to fix this gauge of monofilament— half-inch sections of tube-shaped aluminum into which the newly cut ends of monofilament are shoved and mashed together with a tool called a crimper. The two sections of leaders are crimped together, joined by a small lead swivel. Hook-to-snap assemblies are called leaders, and the men would be busy making them until all three hook boxes were full—approximately three thousand leaders. It was enough work to keep them employed the entire length of the transit to our destination.

While Machado and Tim made leaders, Dave Hiltz worked on ball drops. During fishing, the main line is suspended by flotation that keeps it relatively close to the surface of the ocean. The bullet-shaped Styrofoam floats—or dobs, as some fishermen refer to them—are attached to the main line using snaps, which are fixed to five-fathom pieces of monofilament that act to allow the main line to sink to that depth. The main line needs to be some depth below the surface to avoid some of the part-offs that are often encountered and the spin-ups that can occur when the gear is in the turbulence of waves. Spin-ups, which happen when the leaders and ball drops curl tightly around the main line rather than dangling freely from it, are a time-consuming nightmare. And a part-off, the breaking of the main line in midstring, occurs when the line is crossed by a ship that has a draft deeper than the line's position beneath the surface of the water, or when a shark bites the line in two, or when it's stretched beyond its tensile strength. A typical set is thirty to forty miles of thousand-pound-test mono-filament main line, a thousand leaders, and three hundred floats. So if the gear is constantly spun up and parted off—severed by sharks, ships, or current—you're in for a long, hellish day.

Hiltz measured five-fathom ball drops, pulling mono from a spool hand over hand and stretching it at arm's length, each stretch being six feet, or one fathom. Dave crimped a snap to one bitter end and tied a three-inch eye, or loop, in the other end, into which the floats themselves would be snapped when we set the gear out five days from now. Completed ball drops were cranked onto an aluminum spool, where they are stored when not in use. The main line was stored on its own drum, mounted to the deck just aft of the fo'c'sle and looking like a giant spool of thread with a hydraulic motor on one end. The line would free-spool off the drum when "setting out" (putting fishing gear into the water) and would be "hauled back" (retrieved from the water) hydraulically.

The gear operation closed down when Archie announced that breakfast was being served in the galley. I had eaten frozen pizza nearly every morning for years aboard the *Hannah Boden,* so hot oatmeal was a bonus. We all managed to squeeze in around the tiny galley table, pushing Timmy's bedding into a corner. Tight quarters were further diminished by the size of the men. I was elbow to elbow with Machado and Hiltz. The company was as warm and sweet as the bowl of oatmeal. It hadn't taken long for this crew to develop real camaraderie, I realized as I nearly spit a mouthful of cereal across the table, unable to suppress a giggle at Machado's antics. By the time I had inhaled breakfast, Tim was laughing so hard his face was McIntosh red and Archie was wiping tears from his cheeks. Hiltz sat quietly chuckling and shaking his head.

I hated to leave the breakfast scene. All that good nature, humor, and just plain positivity was magnetic. I had rarely shared a meal with my crew at the galley table in the past. Generally, the conversation was unfit for mixed company. Not to mention the fact that the crew needed time to bad-mouth their captain. But these guys were different. I had certainly shipped with gentlemen before. But not four of them at once. I had always eaten alone in the wheelhouse, paranoid about being away from the radios and missing some critical piece of information that might trickle in. There wasn't much of a trickle happening these days, I knew. There may have been all of one boat out fishing last night. There were two at the dock unloading in Newfoundland and three in transit. Soon there would be more activity to keep track of, and I would need to have all radios tuned and ready. With this in mind, I excused myself from the galley and headed topside to program frequencies into our single-sideband radios.

Scotty had given me a short list of channels to monitor in order to stay up with the small fleet. Standing on my toes, I could just reach the two SSB radios that hung from the overhead behind the chair and above the chart table. Although the radios' manufacturer was I-COM, a maker quite familiar to me, I had no experience with this particular model. Most radios are similar and straightforward in operation, enough so that operating instructions are unnecessary. Or at least that was what I thought when I began pushing buttons. I turned the tuning knobs around and around, scanning the hundreds of preprogrammed frequencies for the ones I needed until my arms were tired of being held over my head. When I couldn't find 3417.0 megahertz on either radio, I decided to program it in. Frustrated after many failed attempts, I began a search for the instruction manual.

I'd been through the steps of programming laid out in the user's guide several times with no luck when Timmy entered the wheelhouse. "Hi. How's it going? Mike is organizing the fish hold and wants me to shut down the ice machine. I think I'll change the oil in the generator. It's almost due," Tim said.

"No." It was a knee-jerk reaction. "Don't shut the ice machine down. What if it doesn't crank back up?" I asked as I continued to push buttons on the starboard SSB. "That would be a real bummer. I'm never comfortable without it running, even if it means shoveling ice overboard to make room for fish. It's a pet peeve of mine."

He sighed. "Yeah, I guess that makes sense. We'll keep stock-piling ice for now. But I'm sure between Archie and me we could always get the ice machine running again if we did shut it down." I liked Tim's confidence. Confidence breeds confidence. But I had cut trips short in the midst of very productive fishing when ice was depleted. Confidence does not erase memory. "Anyway, I heard that having a list was your pet peeve. What are you doing?"

"A list is my other pet peeve," I chuckled. "I'm trying to program this radio. I need a three-megger to communicate with the other boats. I'm following the directions in this manual, but nothing's happening. I've tried both radios," I said as I continued to push buttons.

"Want me to give it a try?" Tim offered.

Normally, I don't allow my crew to touch any of the equipment in the wheelhouse. But, I reasoned, Timmy was a captain. He owned two boats and has skippered some high-end sport-fishing yachts that would certainly put this rig to shame. The *Seahawk* wasn't exactly state-of-the-art technologically. There was nothing on this bridge that was of a hands-off quality. Besides, I was getting nowhere in programming the radios that I desperately needed. "Sure. Thanks, that would be great. I need thirty-four seventeen simplex." So now both Timmy and I scowled at the uncooperative radios and cursed the useless manual. (In all honesty, Tim did not curse.) We tried and tried, Timmy on the starboard and me on the port SSB. I had mistakenly assumed that programming the radios would be easy, and now I regretted not trying it before we departed the dock.

"I got it," Tim whispered.

"Oh, thank God. I was getting nervous about not being able to hear what's going on. What did you do?" I asked.

"I'm not sure." It certainly didn't matter how he'd accomplished programming the radio. But now that it was done, I would leave the starboard radio tuned to 3417.0 for the entire two months so as not to have to rely on Timmy's stumbling across the right combination of buttons again. I thanked him and agreed that it was a good idea to do his engine-room maintenance while the weather was good. And before he disappeared, I reiterated my phobia about running out of ice. Tim assured me that as soon as he was done with the generator, he would resume the ice making. It sure was nice to have someone taking responsibility for the engine room without having to be told when to do things. I was absolutely confident in Tim's mechanical ability and knew that Archie would be overseeing everything, too. I was lucky to have this crew. In the past, although I invariably shipped with a designated engineer, I had always been the best aboard. Trying to do everything aboard a boat was something that I now knew was a function of youthful stubbornness, or paranoia. I had found it difficult to delegate in the past and realized that doing so now would make me a better captain. Confidence in the ability of my crew would allow me to excel in my position of leading them.

I spent the hours between breakfast and late afternoon reading manuals, trying to get some of the nonfunctioning equipment to come to life, and chasing wires around the wheelhouse. Hands-on was my style for learning, and I had plenty about which to educate myself aboard the *Seahawk*. The boat was old and had miles of power cables, connectors, and cords that all seemed to lead to or come from a major bird's nest of multicolored rubber-coated wires under the forward console. It was the most serious ball of confusion I had ever tried to make sense of, and at one point—after losing track of a cable I was tracing for the third time—I simply sat and laughed. In my younger years, I would have ripped the mess out and thrown it all overboard in a fit of impatience and suffered the duration of the trip without whatever it was. I didn't feel that urge now.

I supposed that I had enough of the critical stuff working to get by with, and I realized that I'd never even heard of some of the technology I had aboard that didn't work. So things were okay. I could always get by. That was my strength and perhaps my greatest asset. It would have been nice to have all of the latest gizmos and software and feel as though I were on a level playing field with the other boats. But we would persevere with the minimum. We would catch fish the old-fashioned way. That would be very satisfying. The old guys on the old, junky boat would outfish the best of them. I would have to be careful not to allow my confidence in my ability to run wild. Confidence would be healthy if it remained below cocky. I needn't swagger. Now, if I had a bigger boat . . .

Archie came up and announced that he was going to grill steaks for dinner. The weather was too calm to bake chicken, he reasoned. Grilled steak was exciting. I shared this attitude with the rest of the crew. We were all about the food at this point, as was common during a long steam. Once we started fishing, food would become simply a necessity to fill a void. I wouldn't care what we ate, as long as we ate it quickly and meals did not interfere with the work of getting forty miles of gear in and out of the water on a daily basis. My memory was fully engaged when we'd put together the grub list for the trip. I decided that I would eat a can of sardines every day for lunch and maybe a can for an occasional snack. Sardines were quick, easy and multi-weather-condition food. Arch agreed, as did Tim and Dave. We sailed with a hundred cans. And although a hundred cans would not last sixty days if we all actually did eat them every day for lunch, the quantity seemed a little excessive once they were delivered and stowed.

We were only one day out, and so far I hadn't felt like eating sardines and hadn't seen anyone else enjoying them either. But there would be ample opportunity as soon as the wind kicked up to a velocity that would make it impossible for Archie to prepare a real meal. Or if the trip was extended for whatever reason beyond our food supply, we would always have the sardines. I remembered a trip when sardines would have been torn into like a favorite meal. Poor fishing amounted to many more days at sea than I had originally imagined or planned for. The last week of that ill-fated voyage was filled with voids of all kinds. The cigarette smokers tried rolling lint from the clothes dryer, a can of cake frosting was used for coffee sweetener, and I ate codfish gills. This afternoon was a perfect time to light the grill, I agreed.

The sun had traveled to the stern of the boat. I stood on the upper deck behind the bridge and soaked up the last rays while Arch and Machado set up the grill below. Dave and Tim appeared from within the setting house and sat on the fish hold's hatch cover. Dave looked up, smiled, and said, "All I want to do is catch fish." Tim reported progress of eight hundred leaders for the day. Wow, I thought, at this rate we'd be geared up well before we reached the fishing grounds. A pod of large porpoises broke the otherwise flat surface just off our port quarter. They splashed and played, closer and closer until they swam alongside. I'd been wondering for the past ten years how it would feel to be back here, I thought as I watched Archie light the charcoal with a blowtorch. And right now I remembered at least part of what I'd missed about this industry. The confidence to command is powerful. To command a bunch of screwups is one thing. But to be a leader of real men is dumbfounding.

Archie cocked his head slightly to one side, listening to something. I imagined he heard the high-pitched squeal of the porpoises. He looked up with wide blue eyes, cupped a hand to his mouth, and yelled, "Shut the engine down! Quick!" He and Tim ran toward the fo'c'sle and disappeared. I flew to the controls, pulled back the throttle, threw the engine out of gear, and hit the kill switch. I took a deep breath and held it for a few seconds. I knew I had to join Arch and Tim in the engine room. I glanced out the back door where our wake had run off to the side and petered out. If being at sea is more of a feeling than a place, being adrift is a really bad feeling.

CHAPTER 4

Things Fall Apart

My descent into the engine room was accompanied by stomach-knotting, nearly nauseating anxiety. Fear of what I might find mounted with every step I took down the gangway. When I landed on the steel-plated deck, my field of vision was filled from frame to frame with backs and elbows. Archie and Tim were leaning over and on the engine, their combined mass dwarfing what I would otherwise describe as a hulking machine. I walked around the men's backsides to the opposite side of the engine room, where I could now see the top of the Cummins diesel as well as the men's faces. Arch pulled a long dipstick from its skinny tube, flipped his reading glasses from forehead to bridge of nose, and checked the oil level. He wiped the stick on his shirt, pushed it back into the engine, and withdrew it again to inspect. He gave a satisfied look and returned the dipstick to the tube. Arch squinted over his glasses and focused above my shoulder at the box with the Murphy switch that indicated the coolant level. I looked, too, and seeing nothing out of the ordinary, turned my attention back to the top of the engine.

Tim held a small electronic temperature gauge that he passed along head cover to head cover. He hesitated, showed the reading to Archie, and frowned. "This one is hot!" he yelled to me over the din of the generator. A bead of sweat trickled down Tim's temple and dripped onto the collar of his navy blue shirt.

"I heard a rapping sound. Let's start her up and listen," Arch suggested. I agreed that I would like to hear what had set the big man into fluid, amazingly fast motion, and I walked carefully over to the remote starter, forward of the engine. I reached above my head to the ignition switch, looked for a nod from the men indicating that they were ready, and pushed the toggle up with my thumb. The diesel started without a hitch and ran smoothly at idle. Tim nudged the throttle arm up a bit, and we all listened nervously. Another 100 rpm resulted in a definite and sickening knock. Tim pulled the throttle back to dead idle, and Arch drew a finger across his throat as a signal for me to cut the engine, which I did. I went sort of numb at this point. "The noise seems to be coming from that hot cylinder head!" Arch yelled above the painful, steel-ringing-in-steel clatter coming from the generator. Tim nodded agreement, pursed his lips in concentration, and went to the toolbox.

Two long minutes later, Tim had the cover off the cylinder head that had produced the knock, exposing a series of rusted engine parts. "I thought this engine was just rebuilt. It looks like it was full of water at one time." Tim's disgust clearly pierced the din of our surroundings. "Here's the problem," he added, pointing at the arch-shaped chunk of steel known as the bridge, which supports the rocker arms. "This is loose. Look, this arm fell off to the side and was banging against the cylinder housing instead of the top of the piston. Jim Budi said this engine had just been rebuilt. Pretty sloppy!"

"Can you fix it?" I asked.

"We can put it back together. But we don't have a torque wrench or feeler gauges," said Arch. "I guess we can't make it any worse, and we can't run it the way it is. But these straight-six Cumminses are great engines, and easy to work on." Tim and I agreed that trying to fix the problem, even if the attempt failed, was better than doing nothing, and he and Arch went to work at their best guessing for torque, spaces, and lineups of the rusted parts. "These are *all* loose," Arch kept repeating, shaking his head in disbelief. There was a lot of conversation speculating on the condition of the parts that were used in the rebuild and the haste with which the job must have been done on the boat away from the docks. I tried not to contribute much in the way of bitching, but I was with the men in spirit in my total dismay at our present situation. I prayed that the engine would be fine to run slowly so that we could make landfall under our own steam and avoid the dreaded tow.

The engine compartment's noise and heat finally sent me topside for a breath of air and a look around to ensure that we weren't in the path of any oncoming traffic. Hiltz and Machado stood in the entryway at the main deck level. They had listened to the shouted conversation that had risen with wafts of heat and fumes from below, so they knew all that there was to know. "It looks a little crowded down there, but if you need help, we're here," said Machado. "The engine room ain't my thing."

"Thanks. I don't think there's anything you can do. Tim and Arch have it under control. I'm going up to peek at the radar."

"I just looked," said Hiltz. "There's nothing around. We'll keep a lookout for you. Do we need a tow? Are you going to call Scotty?"

"I'm hoping we can limp to Nova Scotia and not have to bother Scotty. We'll know in a few minutes," I said, and forced myself back down into the uncomfortable heat and noise. The last of Hiltz's mantra about his only desire being to catch fish was quickly drowned by the sound of the generator. I felt like an automaton, going through motions without external motive. I was acting and not reacting. Acting as captain was not the same as *being* captain.

Arch and Tim were both greasy and rusty from fingertips to massive mid-forearms. Tim's usual boyish look had turned to a grimace, and his freckles were lost in redness. Arch appeared unruffled, and this I attributed to his age. Tim tightened the last bolt securing the head cover and gave Arch a look of desperation. "I don't like it," he said.

"I don't like it either," Arch replied. "But it's the best we can do. We don't have the right tools, and we don't know the history here. We can call for a tow, or we can start the engine and hope it's good enough. The engine is already broken, Tim. It's not your fault." Tim nodded and smiled a brief thanks to his friend for removing whatever he was carrying in the way of false responsibility for our troubles.

"Ready to try her?" I shouted. Arch crossed his fingers and

stepped back from the engine. Tim hovered over the work site and chewed his lower lip. I hit the toggle starting the Cummins and listened intently, poised to shut the engine back down if necessary. She sounded good. Could we be this lucky? The prospect of success scintillated in a far corner of my mind. I barely dared to breathe. Tim and Arch got busy with the temperature gauge, checking the six-cylinder heads for any sign of abnormally high readings. Satisfied that everything was okay at idle, I signaled that I was going to the bridge to put the boat in gear and try the engine under a slight load. I hustled up the two flights of stairs while the men took positions to relay verbal commands from wheelhouse to bilge.

I put the boat in gear with every ounce of anticipation in the balance, waiting for an explosion—or nothing. The engine could suddenly seize up, catch fire, or come unglued, I knew. Or it could run smoothly all the way to the fishing grounds and then blow up. Or it could be fine for the next several years. I hoped that Timmy was clear of the engine as I pushed the throttle up a hair. I recalled a generator aboard the *Hannah Boden* that blew up because of lack of oil. A red-hot chunk of steel from the block had flown across the engine room and directly into the engineer's boot, where it traveled down to the top of his foot and burned a deep and dirty hole before he could get the boot off. I yelled to Hiltz to tell Timmy to stand back from the engine and heard the request echo down through the chain of voices before I dared to ease on more throttle.

We were up to 1,100 rpm, and I was as nervous as anyone would be after lighting a fuse and wondering if that particular firecracker would be a dud or a bell ringer. Waiting for an explosion that may or may not happen is a strange feeling, and one that I had never experienced at the hands of my means of propulsion. The tipping point was 1,150 rpm. I hadn't removed my hand from the throttle control when I heard the clatter from below. The knocking was worse this time around, as if someone were inside the engine and trying to get out with a sledgehammer. I heard the screams come up the chain to kill the engine, and I had already done so when the last link yelled, "Shut her down!"

"No shit," I whispered to myself. This was absolutely the worst of all possible scenarios. Twenty-four hours into my epic come-back trip, and here I was, drifting with a blown engine. "Fuck," I said, a little louder.

"We're done, Linny. I guess you better call for a tow," Arch said matter-of-factly. "I have to go down and cheer up the guys. They're all bummed out. Things could be a lot worse. I mean, no one's hurt or dying, right? It's just a machine, and it can be fixed." And his neatly combed blond head vanished as quickly as it had ap-peared, leaving me behind to come to grips with the fact that I had a lot to learn from Archie's reaction and attitude. A much younger Linda Greenlaw would have been enraged at this point and savagely lashing out at anyone and anything. A younger me would throw things and use language that even the crew would find crude. Now I seemed to be adopting a never-let-them-see-you-sweat style of dealing. The out-of-body-experience feeling lingered with the perception of myself as not *doing* anything. Was this a complication that had come with my newfound, mature confidence? I finally resolved that this change was just part of a natural evolution, not a conscious effort to appear cool. I remem-bered the last flat tire I'd had, and knew I hadn't kicked it even without witnesses. Maybe land-based Linda had imprinted onto seagoing Linda.

"*Eagle Eye II, Seahawk.* Pick me up, Scotty?" I called over the SSB radio.

"I'll bet I could!" Scotty's response was quick and cheerful. "What's happenin', Linda? Come on." I quickly explained my situation to Captain Scotty, including the part about needing a tow to Nova Scotia for repairs, and never uttered a foul word. I gave him my present position and distance from Halifax, the closest harbor that I knew would have proper support, which was sixty-two nautical miles to my north. "I'm on my way. I should be to you just before midnight. Have you spoken with Jim or Malcolm? Come on." He asked about contact with the boats' owner and manager. I confirmed that I had not yet delivered the bad news to upper management and would, now that I had lined up a tow. I thanked Scotty profusely before ending my transmission, as I knew how badly he wanted and needed to get his boat to the grounds and begin putting fish aboard.

The ultimate exercise in humility was waiting helplessly for someone to come to your rescue, I realized. The prospect of being on the wrong end of the tow rope was something that I could only think of as complete and total subservience. How could I maintain any illusion of being captainly while in such a state of submission? Because I'd never been in this particular predicament before, I couldn't draw on past experience to know how to feel or what to do or how to act.

Scotty had been a friend for many years. And seeing as both of our boats were owned, at least in part, by the same man, he really couldn't have said no to my request for rescue. I could have called the Canadian coast guard for a tow. But that would have taken longer and been more complicated. And time was money. Every day that we missed fishing was one day closer to the end of the season and one day more beyond the peak moon phase. If we averaged two thousand pounds a day and received four dollars per pound for our catch, we were missing out on eight thousand dollars each day that we were delayed. I was sure that Scotty was capable of doing the same math. Maybe I should have insisted on a mechanic going over the newly rebuilt engine before we left Fairhaven. But we had been in such a hurry to get off the dock with the same calculations and knowing that Scotty was leaving, that thought hadn't crossed my mind. I'd been told that the boat was ready to go fishing, and I had believed it.

I fretted around the wheelhouse for a minute before picking up the satellite phone to call Jim Budi. I remembered, way back, putting off reporting a blown generator engine to its owner for three weeks. Of course, running the generator with no oil had led to that calamity. And I had to accept responsibility for inadvertently pumping all the oil out while the engine was running. Not to mention my part in turning off the low-oil-pressure alarm because the ringing was bothering me, which resulted in bypassing the automatic shutoff. This was much different. I did not feel at all responsible for the *Seahawk*'s present mechanical malfunction. It's just hard to deliver bad news.

I was spared the awkward call when the boat's satellite telephone didn't work. So much of the *Seahawk*'s electronic equipment was outdated, or just plain broken and not repaired, that I wasn't surprised to hear the faint, hollow ringing of dead air in the phone's handset. Archie appeared with his phone just as I was getting ready to radio Scotty and ask that he use his phone to relay my predicament to our shared boss. "Do you need my phone? That thing"—Arch pointed to the boat's phone—"is a piece of junk. Can you believe the engine? That was the only part of the boat I wasn't worried about." Arch screwed the antenna wire into the bottom of the bulky phone and held it out for me to use.

I found Jim Budi's cell-phone number on the margin of the chart where I had scribbled it. I dialed. He answered. I reported. He responded. I hung up. "Jim will call Malcolm, and they'll line up a mechanic and let us know what the arrangements are," I said to Arch. "Scotty will be here in about six hours. The shaft will need to be secured before we get hooked up with the towline," I said, thinking out loud. "Is there any chain aboard?" I asked, knowing that chain was the only reliable way to lash down the propeller shaft to keep it from turning while we were being towed. If the shaft spins without the engine running, there is no oil cooling and lubricating the reverse gear and there is great risk of frying the transmission. We certainly didn't need anything more to keep the mechanic employed or to further delay our fishing trip.

"The guys are searching for chain." I should have known that Arch would already have thought of it. "The coals are perfect. We might as well have dinner. It's a beautiful night." God, I wanted to be as cool as Archie was right now. I agreed that we had nothing else to do until Scotty arrived, and although I had no appetite, I would happily eat steak and try to think of something positive— like the weather.

By the time I had taken two bites of my meal, all the positive conversation had been exhausted, making the food hard to swallow. Even Archie had engaged in, and seemed to rather enjoy, bashing the mechanic, Malcolm MacLean, Jim Budi, and Malcolm's son Putnam, whom the guys had tagged with the name Putz. Complaints were numerous, wide-ranging, and totally warranted. Because they were raging mad, there was a no-holds-barred attitude in my crew's conversation, and I learned a few things that the men had perhaps sheltered me from during our happier, albeit short, past. Among other niceties, I was informed that the vessel of which I was in command was now known among the crew as the *Shithawk*.

The men were discouraged, and why wouldn't they be? I felt as broken as the engine. But the difference was that I was putting on a "bright side" face. I knew from past experience that if I showed my true colors, I would not stop at verbal abuse. A fire ax once thrown through a television screen flashed in my memory. No, I couldn't go there. I really had to make a conscious effort not to join the ranks of despair and to hope that the crew would soon follow suit. Leading by example had always worked in the past. But would the crew follow a phony? I wondered. Because all I had to do was wait helplessly for a rescue, I had nothing to lead them toward but a good attitude while we waited. I'd said before that fishermen have two ways of talking about bad situations: "This sucks" and "This *really* sucks." Well, this really sucked. The confusion created by the conflict between inward toil and outward calm resulted in my feeling like a total android.

I spent the dinner hour running back and forth between the galley and the wheelhouse, like a toy on a string, reporting no news to the crew. Scotty had radioed to tell me that he was communicating with Malcolm, as the boss could not get through to me on the *Seahawk*'s satellite phone. This suited me fine, as I really had no control over the arrangements and had no real opinion other than that I hoped we would not be laid up at the dock for long. This did not need to be voiced, as I knew it was in everyone's best interest to get our show back on the road as quickly as possible. At the very end of the line of decisions, opinions, and communication, I felt that this was the beginning of the end for my captaincy. I felt the burden of responsibility to my crew more than ever. I knew they were doing the math in their own heads and feeling gloomy about opportunities being missed, financial ones as well as life experiences.

Our schedule hinged on how serious the damage was to the engine and how accessible parts would be. I recalled a total rebuild on the *Hannah Boden*'s main engine done in San Juan, Puerto Rico, and a generator repair I endured aboard the *Gloria Dawn* in Provincetown, Massachusetts. In both cases my crew was virtually ready for detox by the time we were back under way, and we had been forbidden by officials to return to either harbor. Both of these episodes were the sort that created sleepless nights. I didn't mention these stories to my crew. But my experiences with repairs in ports other than the vessel's home were uniformly long and unpleasant. Every day we spent at the dock was another day further off the moon we'd be when we got fishing. I didn't mention that to my crew either. I didn't need to, I realized as I listened to the tales of woe coming from around the galley table. The men all had similar catastrophic experiences and seemed to be engaged in a game of one-upmanship, swapping stories that grew in anguish as they proceeded. When I could no longer bear the hangdog faces, I reminded the group that we should be ready to receive the towline before Scotty arrived.

The securing of the shaft became an ordeal unto itself. Rather than a small chore you do in preparation to be towed by another vessel, it was our entire world. There wasn't chain, there was chain, there wasn't enough chain, there was too much chain. . . . We could jam pipe wrenches onto the shaft, no we couldn't, yes we could, watch this, it didn't work. . . . Okay, we'll use the chain. There were no shackles, there were shackles, there was nothing to shackle to, the shackles were too large for the chain. . . . The shackles could be ground to size, no they couldn't, the grinder didn't work, Arch fixed it, no he didn't, yes he did. . . . Another shackle could be stolen from the end of a stay wire, no it couldn't, yes it could. . . . It would be dangerous, no it wouldn't, the weather will be good, what if it isn't? "Tim is an idiot." "Dave doesn't know what he's doing." "I will not be responsible if this doesn't work." "Someone's gonna get hurt if that thing lets go." "He's a jerk." "He's a *fuckin'* jerk."

"Now, you've got the shaft all secure, right?" Scotty asked over the radio as he approached from the northeast.

"Roger, Scotty. We're all set here. Thanks for coming to help. I really appreciate it and will gladly return the favor anytime. Over."

"I know that, Linda. Let's hope you don't have to. Come on!" Scotty was professional and gracious. The assistance he was providing would not only screw up his schedule but would cost him fuel and fishing time. It might cost him the most sought-after berth on the fishing grounds if this delay allowed another competitor to slip in before Scotty arrived. Yet he didn't mention it. For that I was grateful. I could not recall ever feeling so humble. Although fitting, it wasn't a feeling that I enjoyed. In fact, I much preferred pride. But at the moment I had nothing to be proud of.

It was just midnight when the lights I'd been watching on the horizon grew into the silhouette of the *Eagle Eye II*. The weather was still enough for Scotty to maneuver into place without waiting for the help of daylight. My crew stood on the bow, braced to receive a tag line from Scotty's partial crew who were in the stern of their boat ready to toss it. I watched helplessly through the wheelhouse windows as their stern swung around directly in front of my bow. The line was tossed and caught. My crew pulled, hand over hand, until the double-ended cable bridle came aboard. They quickly drew the ends of the bridle through chocks on either side of the stem and placed both eyes over the bit in the center of the bow. My men left the bow for safety reasons, and I gave Scotty the okay over the radio to tow away.

The slack slowly came out of the line as the *Eagle Eye II* eased a distance of about fifty yards from us. The line tightened, and off we went, still unsure of where Scotty was taking us. As of the last conversation, we were splitting the difference between two ports, knowing that a decision was still in the making as to which we would enter for repairs. I supposed there was no urgency in the details of our destination. We had a minimum of eighty miles to go and were making less than seven knots. So I had at least ten more hours to think. I sat back in the captain's chair and stared at the stern ahead of me as it bobbed slightly up and down in the shallow swells. Outwardly I displayed the apathy of a casual bystander. I yawned. Beneath the surface, emotions roiled.

Being on this end of the tow rope was disheartening. It was demeaning. It represented the total antithesis of what I was about.

Independence, self-reliance, and strength shrank as the strain on the line between the two boats grew. Captain of what? The *Shithawk*. My mood wasn't made any lighter by the bickering that rose from below. The crew sounded like young brothers in the backseat on a long car ride. I didn't much like fishing right now.

One by one the men came topside under the guise of offering to stand a watch. But what was clear to me was that they were really coming to get information that I could not provide—where were we going? Or they came to lament our joint baneful existence. One at a time, they hashed over every tiny thing that they had endured at the hands of Jim Budi, Malcolm, and Putz. No longer in command of my ship, I had become a middle manager with the hooking up of the towline. The litany of problems aired ran the gamut from work with no pay to expired dates on batteries. The complaints were getting paltry when Machado ran out of breath at the condition of the paint on the deck. I'd mention it to Jim Budi, I promised. I had heard from everyone except Archie. I didn't know what to do other than listen and show some compassion by agreeing with all they said. If I'd felt like their captain, rather than someone manning a barge, perhaps I would have put an end to what was sounding more and more like nothing more than bellyaching. If I'd been under my own steam, I would have responded to complaints with "Suck it up," "Toughen up," or "Shut the fuck up." Maybe I had softened in the last decade.

Was my present mood a form of grace under pressure? Or was this newfound diffidence a result of the natural process of aging? There was a certain inconsistency, to boot. As thrilled as I'd been with my crew just a few short hours ago, I was now second-guessing my own choices. Perhaps my first thought should have been to hire a seasoned diesel mechanic. Maybe having friends as subordinates (and perhaps insubordinates) was a bad idea. How could I possibly chew them up and spit them out? How could I savagely berate them with one of my earsplitting, foulmouthed rants, known to make grown men wish they'd never been born? Who could I take my frustrations out on? Would any of that make me feel more in command? Being on the wrong end of a towrope zaps a gal's resolve. I sat and stared at the stern ahead of us for what seemed like hours, listening to the voices from down in the galley. I couldn't hear words. The tone was hostile. The laughter was cynical. Maybe I would have been better off with a bunch of idiots as crew, instead of these nice, smart, capable men. I knew how to handle idiots.

I wondered about my present feelings of uselessness and hoped they would soon pass. Perhaps jumping back into this world after such a long absence had been a mistake. I hadn't grown gracefully into this role of the more mature, rational captain. It was more like an abrupt dropping in from another era through some evil time warp. My words and actions were numb, mechanical contrivances. And nobody cared. Surely I had been aware that there were problems inherent in returning to this profession that I had known only as a younger woman. But I hadn't anticipated these heavy feelings that were perhaps born of my absence. Going fishing had always been so carefree in the past. It had always been a financial gamble in which losing had no real consequence other than pride. I'd never had a mortgage when I fished before. Everything I'd owned could be shoved into a plastic garbage bag and slung onto the deck from the back of a truck. And what about my responsibility for Sarai? I was indeed putting her security in jeopardy. Sure, we wouldn't starve to death if this ended badly. But there were things I wanted to be able to do for her and give her that were possible only with adequate income. Most important, I wanted Sarai to believe in me and be able to count on me. I had lived a fairly selfish life before Sarai made her entrance. I didn't want to let either of us down.

"Hey, Linny! Wow, he's towing us along pretty good," Arch said as he entered the wheelhouse. "What are we making, six knots? Not bad."

"I won't know where we're going until morning," I said, anticipating the question.

"It doesn't make any difference to me where we get fixed up." Arch smiled. "I'm not the one quitting and going home."

CHAPTER 5

Adrift

Attrition, a fancy word for jumping ship, didn't usually begin this early in a trip. But so far this trip was anything but usual. I had to consider the fact that this was the earliest opportunity to lose crew that I had ever experienced. It is not unheard of for a man to have a sudden change of heart about fishing in general and to beat feet when a boat hits the dock. But the boat isn't supposed to hit the dock after just forty-eight hours at sea. And we hadn't set even a single hook yet. No one had real reason to be alarmed or any inkling that paychecks would be scarce or thin. This was so premature and unwarranted that I would have to consider it a bailing out rather than a graceful exit.

I recalled a similar situation aboard the *Gloria Dawn*. The mate came up to the wheelhouse, as Archie had just done, and announced that one man was considering hitting the road. I fired the entire crew in an instant, mate and all. Looking back, I could now see that I'd been extremely impetuous. Being stupid and counterproductive had never fazed me before. The mass firing had been a matter of principle. But now I couldn't remember *which* principle. I didn't have it in me to be so brash any longer. It would be much smarter to be composed and calculated and less spontaneous. "Who's quitting?" I asked calmly.

"Machado is sitting with his cell phone and waiting for coverage. He says he has bad vibes and wants to cut his losses. Dave may follow him," Arch had confided, in what I knew was sincere concern for how abandonment might affect me emotionally. Little did my friend know about me. I would nip this in the bud.

"I can't say as I would blame them if they headed home. Please find out what their intentions are so that I can line up a couple of guys. We can't waste time at the dock waiting for crew. We've got fish to catch!"

"Yeah." Arch paused to think. "Yeah, you're right. I know a great guy who will jump on a plane headed *anywhere* to go fishing. Want me to call him? I can call Marge and have her arrange flights. In fact, I know two guys. I should call them now and put them on standby. Want me to?"

"I have a list of guys in mind who wanted to come if I had room for them. I didn't then. Now I do. I assumed that Machado and Tim would be the guys bailing out. Hiltz is a surprise," I said.

"Tim is here for the duration. Don't you worry about him. He's solid. As long as I stay, he stays. And I'm not going anywhere until you do. Machado is sort of miserable, and I think he's making Dave nervous."

I knew well, from experience with hundreds of hired hands in the past, how infectious attitudes are—how one negative influence could impel an otherwise complacent member of a crew to ditch. And perhaps that knowledge had led to as many firings. It's much better to terminate one man's position than to lose two quitters. There's too much time to think while a boat is steaming. Too much rack time, too much idle time, and too much time to sit around the galley table acting as "fo'c'sle lawyers" (as my old mentor Alden Leeman had always referred to the malcontents) never resulted in the development of positive attitudes. One disgruntled man could plant a seed, and downtime—especially like this—could nurture the most fragile point of strife to full-grown petulance. Like bedsores, small complaints fester and spread with a little agitation and chafing. Putting salve on bedsores had never been my method.

"Someone aboard here is a Jonah!" I said, referring to what mariners consider a person who brings bad luck to a boat. "It's got to be Machado or Hiltz. Can you get confirmation *now* that they're quitting?" I asked, as optimistically as I could, knowing that Arch would see through my psychology but would also go along with it in trying to call a bluff. "I really need to know how many replacements to get." Being called a Jonah was a real slap in the face. Now the ball would be in someone else's court. I may have forgotten a lot in the last ten years, but the basic game was still the same. And I believed that I was still the reigning champ of head games played at sea. "I'll keep my fingers crossed that they'll both go home."

And with that, Arch essentially took on the role of first mate. He became the go-to and the go-between, effectively relieving me of running up and down between three decks. Archie carried out my wishes and orders even when he disagreed with them. Now he went below and returned with the anticipated results. No one was quitting. We were all in, from dock to dock, as they say. "Oh, that's too bad," I said. "I don't suppose I have grounds to fire either of them. They haven't actually done anything wrong yet." Arch was quick to agree that I certainly could not fire anyone. But I knew he would smoothly slip that concept into his next visit to the galley table.

I sounded like a bitch, but this was actually one of many mind games that fishermen, and men of the sea in general, play to occupy nonworking hours. I preferred having the men nervous about the security of their jobs to me worrying that they were quitting, and scrambling willy-nilly for adequate understudies. This was a lot more entertaining than measuring the depth of dips the stern of the *Eagle Eye II* made with each bob, which was the only other amusement I had. This drama had real potential. The theatrics inherent in life in a small, tight-knit island community had nothing on life aboard a commercial fishing boat. I knew that as soon as we all got busy going about our business, things would be A-OK. We would be so busy working once the engine was fixed that the games would be delayed until the next dull moment. This was just like home.

In spite of the men's multiple offers to take watches, I stayed up all night. It wasn't until Scotty called the next morning and said that he was delivering us to Sambro, Nova Scotia, that I gave in to boredom more than sleepiness and went to my bunk. We were fighting a bit of tide and would, according to Scotty, arrive outside Sambro Harbor that evening at around ten. At that time we would drop the tow and pick up lines from a Canadian coast guard vessel that would escort us right to the dock, where a certified Cummins mechanic would be waiting. With a solid plan in place and everything seemingly organized, I managed to get a bit of sleep, waking to the sight of a thin, gray line of land off on the distant horizon.

Just before 10:00 P.M., we dropped Scotty's towing bridle from our bow. And like a dog suddenly liberated from a taut leash, he was gone without so much as a whimper, free of the sixty-three-foot hunk of steel that he'd been tethered to for nearly twenty-four hours. Adios, amigo, I thought, and imagined that his reply would have been more of a good riddance—and rightfully so. As the lights of the *Eagle Eye II* disappeared behind a headland, a sharp twinge of anxiety swept over me quite unexpectedly. Depending on how long we were laid up, Scotty would be gaining a real advantage. He'd certainly reach the grounds before I did, giving him first dibs on the water. He might make several sets before we arrived and have part of a trip aboard before we landed a single fish.

The old familiar wheels of competition had begun to turn. My competitive spirit in the past had always been driven by hunger. "A hungry dog hunts harder" is what Alden used to say. Now, it wasn't exactly the case with me that I actually wouldn't eat if we came up short on the catch. My hunger wasn't literal. I wanted to be on the water for many reasons—not just financial. I wondered if competition just for the sake of it would be enough to drive me now. The only thing I really had at stake was my reputation. My crew would not suffer unduly without huge paychecks. I reminded myself that I had never fished for the money. I fished for the love of it, and I imagined that the competition was part of what I loved.

But, I realized, I had never fished when I wasn't living from hand to mouth. Desperation was always good motivation, but it came at a price. Some part of me was glad to know that it wasn't life or death, but another part of me was relieved to feel the burning in my stomach when I thought of Scotty getting such a jump on me. The desire to outfish my comrades came quite naturally. I felt myself slipping into the comfort of more familiar ground, less *acting* and more *being* captain. I wished the Canadians would hurry up.

The small powerhouse of a vessel out of Sambro was manned by several Canadian coastguardsmen. The warning-orange boat was alongside and throwing lines to my crew before my impatience could be verbalized. Secured to the *Seahawk*'s hip, or made fast to our port aft quarter, the smaller boat had no trouble manhandling her incapacitated rescuee. Absolutely smooth and professional, Canadian mariners were among the best in the world, I had always believed. The Nova Scotian captain really put on a show at the wharf. A couple of thrusts of his engines and there we were, without creating so much as a ripple. Dock lines were heaved to men waiting to receive them. The towboat cut loose and pulled away to its berth across the harbor.

Among the guys on the dock stood a tall, gray-haired gentleman wearing a jumpsuit. A large steel toolbox rested at his feet. "You must be the Cummins man," I said, looking up from the deck.

"I am." And that was the end of the dialogue. Timmy helped the mechanic aboard by grabbing the box of tools, and they both disappeared through the entryway and down into the engine room.

I was greeted by a cheery man in a wheelchair who introduced himself as my port agent. His last name was Henneberry, familiar to me as a family of highliners, or top-notch producers, on the international fishing scene. The tide was low enough to prohibit me from climbing up or him from sliding down. So I reached to shake his hand and receive some paperwork required by customs and immigration. "Just fill in the blanks, and I'll be around tomorrow to pick them up," he said. I thanked him, bade him a good night, and headed for the warmth of the galley, where I spread the forms on the table.

The same basic immigration and customs forms I had filled out time and again when entering any foreign port, they mainly asked for names and passport numbers. We had no booze or guns. Machado was our only smoker, and he claimed three cartons, which were supposed to be kept in a locked compartment. The process was laid-back relative to what happens in larger ports.

After supplying me with his passport information, Machado requested permission to leave the boat. He had a friend on the dock and had been invited to "go out." This "going out," in my vast past, had often led to nothing good. But I really couldn't tell a forty-year-old man that he was grounded. He promised to be back aboard first thing the next morning and was gone. I was a little nervous about the games I had dabbled in earlier and sincerely hoped that Machado wasn't headed for the airport in Halifax. He'd certainly get the last at-bat if that were the case. I wished that I trusted Machado. He had given me no reason to distrust him, but I didn't know him well. What I did know, or at least believed, was that he was smart in a streetwise way about the ropes, hoops, and loopholes in the unwritten rules engaged in by captain and crew in what sometimes is more of a battle than what is normal in conventional working relationships. Compared with Machado, the rest of the crew were naïve in the ways and wiles of this salty workaday world. Liking Machado was not a struggle. He was eminently likable. There was just a little something there—a cleverness that put me on edge—that I found challenging. His range of experience in commercial fishing put him in my league. He might even have a few moves I hadn't encountered. And if Machado outfoxed me, it would cost some time. Lost time would equate to Scotty's getting more of a head start on his trip. I couldn't have that.

Archie and Hiltz seemed content to hang around the galley with me. We listened to Timmy screaming over the generator and were amused that there was never any response from the mechanic. "Maybe he's using sign language," Arch suggested. Hiltz nodded and flipped a double bird. This seemed very funny at the time. We laughed hysterically until tears formed. Looking back, it doesn't seem a bit humorous. But I'm sure that we were stressed to the point of silliness and needed some comic relief. And Machado, who was our usual supply of jokes, had left us to our own devices. When the weight of anticipation got to be too much for me and my belly ached from laughing, I reluctantly decided to descend to the engine room to check on progress and hear the prognosis.

Before I made it halfway down the stairs, I met Timmy coming up. Glad to put distance between me and the noise again, I hurried back to the galley with Timmy close on the heels of my rubber boots. "How's it looking?" I asked.

"The mechanic is great," Tim said as he wiped sweat from his forehead with a paper towel. "So far he's found two bent push rods that appear to have been caused by the hasty rebuild. Every bolt securing rocker arms had backed out to finger tight. It's a wonder we didn't trash the entire engine."

"So we *didn't* trash the entire engine?" I asked nervously.

"No. He's still checking, measuring, tightening—but I think we'll be fine. He brought rods, and so far he hasn't found anything that will keep us from getting back out tomorrow. Or is it today now? It's a good thing we didn't run the engine any more than we did. It could have been a lot more serious." This was the best news!

Archie clearly understood diesel engines as well as Tim did. They theorized on a few points that were slightly beyond my mechanical-engineering acumen. Basically they assumed, based on what had happened, that the mechanic who did the recent work may not have retorqued the bolts after the engine had been put through the usual paces following work that required certain tension strengths to be put on threaded fasteners that hold various engine parts together properly. Once a newly rebuilt engine is brought up to temperature, it's vital to check and retighten as necessary due to the effect of heat on steel. "It's an expanding and shrinking thing," explained Arch.

I was greatly relieved to understand that we would be throwing the lines off the dock at first light. We had certainly lucked out this time. Tim went back to assist the mechanic, while Arch, Dave, and I remained in the galley extolling our good fortune, our great mechanic, and our hardworking shipmate. We wouldn't be far behind Scotty if we could indeed get under way in the next few hours. In fact, with Scotty going to Newfoundland to pick up two crew members, we could actually beat him to the grounds. I had always done what I could to have any perceivable advantage over my fellow captains, and getting first hooks in a certain piece of water that might be more productive than its surroundings would be huge. The North Atlantic Ocean is vast, and there are hundreds of square miles where swordfish can be caught. But there are known hot spots, and I now had a shot at one of them. The ability to get the first set under my belt before Scotty arrived on the scene was within reach, and the prospect of gaining an edge excited me.

I didn't voice any of this to Arch and Hiltzie, as doing so might put me in less than a good light. The more I considered my situation, the better I felt. I'm not proud of these feelings, but there they are. Scotty had just sacrificed this same advantage I sought by doing me a favor. Great! This is a classic example of the thinking that separates fishermen from the rest of humankind. Perhaps my hunger hadn't been sated after all.

The only spoiler to our second auspicious weighing of anchor could be Machado, I reflected while Arch and Dave helped Tim with the tools as the mechanic of few words stretched a long leg across from boat to dock. Mr. Henneberry had come and collected our paperwork for customs. The engine had been given a clean bill of health. We were discharged and had only to wait for Machado to grace us with his presence before leaving Sambro and charging back on course toward prosperity.

We all conceded that we could use some sleep, and with a man still ashore there was no reason not to take a short nap. My errant crew member had been so nonchalant about showing up in Fairhaven to help prep for the trip that I figured there wasn't a chance he'd step aboard at dawn following a night on the town. Shore leave in a foreign port often leads to an attitude of carefree gluttony made easy with the knowledge that anyone you happen upon is a stranger. And how could scandalous words of drunkenness or bad deeds possibly find their way so many miles home, against the tide? These thoughts had led to trouble and, at the very least, to late arrivals with hangovers—it had happened so frequently that I knew I had time to close my eyes for a while before going ashore myself to track down Machado. But I was too wired to sleep, thinking of the miles Scotty had gained already.

Then, just as the crew had turned in, Machado was climbing aboard. "Good morning, everyone!" He appeared to be in great shape considering what I suspected of his overnight activities. Beyond surprised, I was shocked to see him so early. "Hey, you should see the mackerel at my buddy's freezer plant. It's gorgeous!" This was so far from what I expected to hear that I was confused. Had he really spent his night of shore leave checking out bait? "Linda, I know you're not thrilled with the bait we have on board. We can get some great-looking stuff delivered this morning if you want— mackerel or squid." Machado was right regarding my opinion of the ten thousand pounds of frozen mackerel I had reluctantly left Fairhaven with. Most of the fish we had were freezer-burned and on the small side. I had rejected one pallet of bait that was worse than the rest, but I had to take something. Good bait always equals good fishing. "The mackerel is huge!" Bigger bait had always resulted in bigger fish. This would be another, even greater asset than beating the *Eagle Eye II* to the fishing grounds.

"What's the price?" I asked.

"Cheaper than that shit we got in Fairhaven. We can't afford not to take some. And Malcolm has an account in good standing with my buddy. All I have to do is say the word, and he'll be here with whatever you want." Machado held out his cell phone, poised to dial.

He had my interest. I wondered whether it was ethical or within company protocol to take on bait, or any added expense, without permission. As I pondered, I received a gentle reminder of why we were here in the first place. Sure, I thought, I wasn't to blame for the engine problem. And this delay had cost us dearly in time lost toward eventual fishing. The moon was shrinking. Could we swing a double bait bill? No, probably not. Could I turn down perfect bait? No, definitely not.

Another nudge from the peanut gallery convinced me that I was perfectly justified in doing whatever I deemed necessary to give my crew and myself every possible advantage in what hadn't started out real swell. "All right, I would like some decent bait. But we can't afford to toss what we have. And we will certainly be billed for it. How about a thousand pounds of the best and biggest mackerel to supplement what we have already?" This was a fair compromise. Although the crew was tired, they rallied to show sincere enthusiasm for new and improved bait. Machado dialed his friend.

A little while later, a truck backed down the wharf and came to an abrupt stop with a hiss and puff from the air brakes. The men quickly moved the boxes of bait from the back of the truck to the *Seahawk*'s deck. I tore the top of a cardboard box open to inspect the frozen contents. Machado had not exaggerated. Horse mackerel is what we call this size fish at home—and these were horsier than most. Certainly full-figured, they carried their girth from head to tail and must have averaged two pounds each in weight. Rather than the dull haze that older bait of lesser quality shows in its skin, the fish shimmered in black, deep blue, and crisp white. Four grown men stood behind me and admired the frozen mackerel with oohs and aahs more appropriate to a bunch of guys looking at a copy of *Playboy* magazine. When we finished ogling what we imagined would result in some whopper sword-fish, I signed the receipt and went up to the bridge to start the engine in preparation for leaving the wharf. The prospect of having better bait than Scotty was exciting.

The engine warmed as the crew stacked the new bait in the fish hold on a bed of saltwater ice. I booted up a computer and examined the electronic chart of Sambro Harbor that appeared. I hadn't paid strict attention to the way we'd entered the port, as I wasn't driving at the time. But the channel from the wharf looked to be well buoyed, and the conditions were pristine. I'm always a bit apprehensive when navigating in an area with which I'm un-familiar—even with the best electronic aids and paper charts, nothing beats local knowledge. I switched on the radar and the depth sounder.

Then I stepped out the back door and did a quick head count. All present and accounted for; even Machado sat on the rail and smoked a cigarette, waiting patiently for me to shove off. I asked the men to let all the lines go except for the one running aft from the forward bit. I put the boat in gear with the rudder hard to port. The boat strained against the remaining line, springing the stern to starboard and away from the dock. I put the engine in neutral to relieve the tension of the line, nodded to Hiltz to re-lease the spring line, and we were off.

Idling the length of the channel, I kept an eye on the chart plotter and the depth sounder. The area appeared to be idiotproof in its abundance of deep water interrupted by the occasional rocky outcropping or island. The landscape was very much like home, causing slight warmth in this otherwise cool day. Outside the harbor I steered east of a tiny island named Isle of Man and split the difference between Inner Sambro Island and Sambro Island proper. The last peak of ledge protruding through the glassy surface was Gull Rock, which I passed to the north before turning east and getting back on course for the Grand Banks. The only obstacles to stay clear of were the dangerous shoals around two spots marked on the chart—Black Rock and the Sisters—each of which I would give a wide berth.

Land faded as open ocean seemed to embrace the *Seahawk* in her easterly progress. I snapped on the autopilot and sat in the captain's chair, worries dimming with distance gained from shore. Things could have been so much worse. Scotty had taken us in a northeasterly direction to Sambro, so the time under tow had been somewhat productive, as we were closer to our destination now than we had been when the engine broke down. And with the price of diesel fuel at an all-time high, any savings was huge. Repairs to the engine had gone more smoothly than I could have imagined. I had spent too many days in foreign ports waiting for engine parts that always got lost along the way to be anything other than surprised now to be at sea. We had spent only twelve hours at the dock. The crew was intact and already at work making gear. Our time in Nova Scotia had been a touch-and-go landing in terms of boats. And I was in the captain's chair, not a passenger at the end of a towrope.

Conversation on the SSB radio clued me in to the disappointing fact that I would not beat Scotty to the grounds, as his crew members were being delivered to him by another of the Eye Fleet's boats, the *Eyelander*. Captain Swanny was unloading a trip in Bay Bulls, Newfoundland, and was scheduled to leave the dock in time to rendezvous with the *Eagle Eye II* just as it was arriving to make its first set. There goes that edge, I thought. Oh, well, we had a wager for the biggest fish, and I was confident that our mega-mackerel would land a real monster regardless of who was first to get hooks wet. The new bait was our secret weapon. Basic Fishing 101: Great bait and sharp hooks would always outproduce any combination of gadgets and tricks. I knew this and felt it the way devotees feel their religion. I was confident.

The GPS indicated seven hundred miles to go and an average speed of 7.8 knots. In just under four days, I would be scoping out a piece of water. My present destination, marked as a waypoint on the chart plotter, was 44 degrees 30 minutes north latitude and 48 degrees 30 minutes west longitude. This was the general location of what had been reported as the most productive swordfishing so far this season. Once we arrived in the area, I could begin the most important of my responsibilities—putting the gear on the fish. The job of finding the perfect spot to work, based on currents and surface temperature, had always been my forte. I felt my pulse quicken with anticipation. Four nights from this evening, we would be making our first set. I wondered how it would feel to haul the first fish aboard.

At dusk I could smell Marge's chicken recipe. Life was good again. We were on our way to engage in my first love. Mother Nature had been cooperative so far. Even if Murphy's law had flexed a muscle, it had been meager and quickly overwhelmed. After all, conquering obstacles was one of the things that drew me to a life at sea. There was so much satisfaction in persevering through hardship. And there was never an end to the hardship as long as I was aboard a boat. I sometimes felt as though I marked time at sea solving one problem and waiting for the next to materialize. The engine failure was behind us, and any complication that arose now would seem like a snap in comparison.

The sounds from the engine room were muffled when Archie filled the stairway. I knew he was coming to deliver dinner, the aroma of which had piqued my ever-present appetite. "Hi, Arch," I said as his head and shoulders came into view above the top step. "It's another beautiful night!"

Arch rested his massive forearms on the ledge surrounding the stairs. He didn't have my dinner. He held a wrench. "The ice machine isn't working. Salt water is pouring into the fish hold."

CHAPTER 6

Water, Water, Everywhere

I could hear Hiltz shouting. "There's a fucking lot of water down there. Is the pump working? Where's Timmy?"

"Timmaaay!" Arch bellowed from the wheelhouse stairs, loudly enough for Tim to hear in the engine room. Tim replied just as loudly that he was on it.

"The water is up to the second pen board! What the fuck?" Hiltz screamed again.

Arch smiled nonchalantly, shrugged his shoulders, and said to me, "It's not that bad. We're not sinking." I wasn't sure whether my concern should be for the level of water in the fish hold, the fact that the high-water alarm never sounded, or that the ice machine wasn't working. No ice aboard a fishing boat is not like no ice on a picnic. Warm beer and tired salad are no big deal. But no ice-making capability on this trip spelled doomsday like nothing else. We were in the business of providing fresh fish, and that meant packing them in saltwater ice until they went to market. Nonfunctioning ice machines have ended many a fishing trip. No ice, no fish. Lack of ice was indeed a nightmare, and one that would be confronted as soon as we addressed the first priority of dewatering the boat.

Like most shipboard near emergencies, flooded compartments that are normally without water need to be dealt with quickly to minimize damage and danger. The level of danger rises as the water does. In marine stability we have the term "free surface effect," which refers to the sloshing motion of liquid—be it water or fuel or whatever liquid cargo may be on board; when a volume of fluid moves, it changes or exaggerates the motion of the vessel. This can obviously be very dangerous, as it puts the boat in an unstable condition. At around six pounds per gallon, depending on its salinity level, the right amount of water in the wrong place can be disastrous. And for the water to be high enough to cause anyone to make noise about it, I knew there was, as Dave had said, "a fucking lot" of it where it should not be. I also knew that shipboard emergencies test the leadership/teamwork balance aboard, and these areas had always been ones in which I'd excelled. Even when not perilous, hard times in general call for cool heads and cooperation behind whoever takes charge.

Hiltz continued to vocalize with an ever-increasing degree of hysteria while Arch remained calm, almost to the point of worrying me that he wasn't taking the situation seriously enough. I knew that Dave Hiltz had a penchant for melodrama. But Arch was the other extreme. Nothing seemed to shake him.

"I guess I had better take a look. Excuse me, Arch," I said as I squeezed by him and down to the main deck. The cover was off the fish hold's hatch, making it easy for me to assess the water problem. Before looking down, I promised myself to not let whatever I saw put me over the edge. The water was indeed deep enough to raise an eyebrow, but not deep enough to panic me. If the sea state had been anything other than calm, I would have been more upset. It's always disconcerting to be "making water" anywhere other than into the freshwater holding tank, and I hoped that Arch's first analysis had been correct, about the source of the water being the ice maker. Shutting off a valve would shut off the flow. I vowed to remain cool and collected, no matter what.

I'd been in much worse situations. I recalled an all-night bucket brigade to empty a flooded lazarette. Now, that was scary! I had, out of necessity, become part of the human chain of bucket scoopers, passers, and dumpers. Sheer determination (and fear of capsizing) had kept us all going until we got the water down far enough to discover and remedy the problem. Water weighs more than air. Many a boat has rolled over and/or gone to the bottom because an alarm did not work. And, like fire, when water problems go unnoticed long enough, they become difficult, if not impossible, to contain and reverse. There are times when a captain can bark orders and other times when working with the crew, elbow to elbow, is the best way out of a bad situation. I realized that this was something that had not changed since my last trip and in fact never would. I'd be the first to roll up my sleeves when the time came. There was no doubt in my mind that the time would indeed come. I just hoped it hadn't already.

All U.S.-licensed commercial fishing vessels are subject to safety examinations performed by the coast guard and also by surveyors working for marine insurance companies. One of the more critical and elemental parts of maintaining the safety of any boat is to ensure that the alarms are functioning properly. High-water alarms are self-explanatory devices, required in every separate compartment of a ship's hull, that sound an alarm when they become submerged. I figured that the alarms all worked when I saw the safety examiner place a sticker on the *Seahawk*'s windshield showing that the vessel had passed all the tests before we left Fairhaven.

Whatever the alarm situation, I knew that the *Seahawk* had ample and multiple pumping systems to dewater, also required in every compartment. So I was confident that we would soon be riding lighter in the water. Timmy joined me at the hatch, looked down, and confirmed that the water was now receding. He shared and voiced the same concern I had as to why the high-water alarm had not sounded, and he added that we'd been lucky that he'd happened to be going into the fish hold to get Archie a gallon of fresh water (of all things) to make gravy with when he discovered what could easily have become catastrophic if we'd been eating healthier. Thank God for gravy.

"As soon as the hold is pumped out, Arch and I will tackle the ice machine," Tim said.

"Timmaaay!" The accent was on the second, drawn-out syllable as Arch hailed his friend in what was becoming his signature call. Tim hustled in the direction from which his name had come and met Arch beside the ice machine, while I stared at the bottom of the fish hold's ladder watching the sloshing salt water slowly disappear below the deck plates. I figured that the beds of ice had been partially washed out as well as some of what we had stockpiled in two aft pens, or bins. Ice-machine malfunction is perhaps the second-biggest frig (a term used in coastal Maine having nothing to do with copulation, but rather meaning a nuisance) hampering commercial fishermen, following closely the loss of propulsion, like what we had just experienced. We were not in any danger. But without ice we don't fish. So remedying the machine failure that had caused the flood in the fish hold was imperative. Without the ice maker in full production, there was no point in proceeding to the fishing grounds. Ice can, in extreme circumstances, be transferred from vessel to vessel using baskets. But these occasions are always if the boat in need is at the end of a trip, when its ice-making capabilities are lost. Inconveniencing the donor vessel is a one- or possibly two-shot deal in dire situations. There is just no way anyone would agree to keep us in ice for an entire trip. I had faith in Tim and Arch. But that devotion did little to soothe the burning in my abdomen as I considered the possibility of yet another detour to Nova Scotia.

The ice maker had, like the main engine, just been worked on at the dock prior to our departure. The refrigeration guys had spent the better part of three days troubleshooting when they finally discovered that two hoses (intake and discharge) had been reversed. Of course, by that time they'd replaced every conceivable problematic part in a process of elimination. We were thrilled with the abundance of new parts thrown at the problem before finding the hose reversal, and the machine had made great ice until just a short while before. I now hoped Tim and Arch could pull a rabbit from a hat and, to mix my metaphors, keep us from becoming Nova Scotia's newest bad penny.

I poked my head around the side of the setting house, where

Hiltz had returned to work building leaders with Machado. "What the fuck, Skip?" Hiltz asked, with wide eyes and arms open to either side, palms up in question.

"The tide is going out. Don't worry, Dave," I said, hoping to calm his agitated nerves.

"I'm not worried. All I want to do is catch fish."

"In that case I'd be worried." I chuckled as I left the stern and heard the men laugh behind me. They didn't call us the *Shithawk* for nothing. As I marched the length of the deck, I could see that my team of engineers had the ice machine surrounded. I elbowed my way between the men to observe that they had the refrigeration gauges in place, connecting the compressor to a bottle of refrigerant. The small, round sight glass that functions to indicate when there is unwanted air in the system, or lack of refrigerant, showed an abundance of bubbles.

"I don't know what caused it, but some refrigerant seems to have escaped. We can't find a leak," said Arch. "Don't worry, we'll have it back up and making ice before the chicken dries out." Timmy didn't look as optimistic but didn't say anything that might contradict his friend. I left the men charging the drum-shaped machine and returned to the wheelhouse to begin the depressing act of figuring distance and time to a variety of ports along Canada's southern coast. I scanned the chart. It was clear that the most convenient stop for repairs would be the tiny island of Saint-Pierre.

Saint-Pierre and Miquelon, two lone islands claimed and owned by France, lay just thirty-two nautical miles south of Newfoundland. I had been to Saint-Pierre a number of times in the past when Canada first shut down its cod fishery and thought it prudent not to allow foreign vessels to resupply in Canadian ports while the native fishermen were out of work. The French didn't seem to mind taking our money, I recalled. Saint-Pierre is, of course, French for St. Peter, one of at least six patron saints of fishermen, a number I've always found telling. A trip to Saint-Pierre to fix the ice machine would be the least painful as far as lost time. I would hardly have to change course. And we would be closer to our targeted destination than a return to Sambro or a steam to any port in Newfoundland would take us.

I sat and thought about the prospect of having repairs done in that all-French-speaking place with only English spoken aboard the *Seahawk*. I had always gotten by in the past. But I'd never needed anything more than fuel and groceries. "Petrol" was universal, as were hand motions to the mouth to indicate food. I remembered the quaintness of the island and how it reminded me of home. I recalled that Saint-Pierre also owned the distinction of being the only place in North America to have used the guillotine, and I wondered why this was the single fact I could bring to the surface from the depth of ten years.

I tweaked the autopilot a few degrees to the north on the outside chance that news from below would soon lead me in that direction. Saint-Pierre was a neat place. It had always appealed to me in a "Gee, I sure would like to come here sometime for a vacation rather than as a necessity to get supplies for work" sort of way. Even the time zone was unique! Three hours behind Greenwich mean time, two hours ahead of eastern standard, one hour ahead of Halifax, and thirty minutes off Newfy standard made this island more islandlike than any other landmass surrounded by water to claim the title. It might be fun to go there, if we had to go.

Who was I kidding? Myself? The truth is that I would feel like a total loser if we had to go to any port for any repairs. The next port of call for the *Seahawk* had to be Bay Bulls, Newfoundland, with a boatload of fish to unload.

As it turned out, all this psyching myself up to be delayed was for naught. Tim was gleeful in his exclamation that he and Arch had been successful in fixing the ice machine, which was now "up and making better and more ice than ever." The weight of pending failure left my back and shoulders as I changed course back toward our original waypoint. I felt as though I had dodged a bullet and could now abandon the defensive stance I had assumed and stand tall. I prepared myself to hear alarms as Timmy warned me that he would be testing them all right away. Arch delivered the chicken dinner, complete with stuffing and lots of gravy. Life was good again.

In what was now becoming a familiar kind of internal ritual, I realized that I hadn't reacted to the ice-machine problem in the same way that I would have in my younger days, and I couldn't help questioning why. I had this ten-year increase in age lurking around my psyche and taking responsibility for everything I did, said, or didn't do or say. I couldn't imagine having one of my old hissy fits now. I didn't want to be thought of by my crew as a screaming idiot who rants and raves in the face of adversity. I didn't want to act like a tyrant. I had always spoken of working *with* my crew rather than them working *for* me. That is how I truly felt, and feel. It went beyond simple syntax. I hoped that the occasional outbursts I was capable of had indeed become a thing of the past—written off as youthful foolishness—and were not playing hide-and-seek. I knew that I was a real team player. I knew that I had an uncanny ability to buckle down when necessary. That quality hadn't come aboard this trip, nor had it been swept out with the ebbing tide of other things that recede with age. I guessed it didn't matter why, and I hoped that the anger management would continue through what was feeling like a series of personal tests studding this extended shakedown cruise.

Forty-eight hours of one thing after another had pushed me to the limit. When the wind picked up a bit, causing a healthy sea, it became clear that the stay wires securing the outrigger booms were too loose. Turnbuckles were tightened to their maximum, or "two-blocked," as we say, and still the wires were slack enough to allow the booms to wag. Links of chain were removed, and shackles were interchanged until the best combination possible was achieved. When spray became green water taken over the bow, the troughs formed by the sides of the house and the top of the gunwales became sluiceways through which rivers ran. It rained salt water in the engine room. Dripping water over the heat from the engines created briny stalactites that grew down from the overhead like icicles, creating new work for Timmy in their removal. The camper-style toilet in the head leaked water. The generator leaked fuel. Even the electricity leaked somehow, causing static interference in all the electronics.

The computer quit. The radar quit. Dave Hiltz quit every time something else failed. Things were breaking, sometimes two at once. When it seemed we were outnumbered, we dropped into zone defense. Whoever had expertise or energy to tackle the job became point man, with the four others solidly behind, helping where needed. When the problems slowed to a trickle, we went back to one-on-one, every man covering his own territory. We held team meetings at the galley table to discuss strategy for defense in the next attack, something that flew in the face of what I had always maintained: that a commercial fishing vessel is not a democracy. We planned offense—sometimes a gang tackle, sometimes more of a tag team—to get through the daily chores beyond repairs. The *Shithawk* had us on our heels, but we continued to move ahead.

The beeper buoys were a mess. Two of their canisters were full of water. One had half an antenna. One had no antenna. One had a full antenna but no electronic board. Two had faulty switches. One had a frozen switch. The "real gem," according to Archie, was the buoy with no buoyancy, no batteries, and a cracked canister. We actually stood around that buoy and marveled at how and why it had remained aboard the boat. We were now at the point of laughing at each piece of equipment as it fell. And they fell like dominoes. Deck lights became disco blinkers when the boat rolled just right. We rewired, replaced, and refitted where we could. Where we could not, we placed bandages and secured blowout patches and jury-rigged until it seemed there was nothing left to go wrong. How many times did I hear Tim say, "It's fixed. I think we're okay now"? His words soon became known as the kiss of death. In the few moments that we relaxed, we sat and waited for the next thing to break, leak, or malfunction. We hung strong as a unit in spite of the *Seahawk*'s efforts to divide and conquer. I didn't have the energy to fly off the handle.

Archie became known as "Archie Bungee," for the number of bungee cords he stretched around the boat. Two-part epoxy formed patches until the *Seahawk* looked like she had broken out with a strange rash. He seemed to have an endless source of bungees and personal first-aid supplies. Bungees and Liquid Skin were like weeds. Archie had put the end of his thumb back together after a mishap with a knife, had glued together a gash on his forearm that otherwise would have needed stitches, and had filled a hole he'd acquired in falling onto the stove in a rough head sea that sent him for a loop—all with the amazing bandage in a bottle. He swore by the stuff, and we all agreed to buy stock in Liquid Skin should the fishing trip not pan out favorably in our financial interest.

When the water maker bit the dust, I struggled to keep my cool. I ran into a knot before I reached the end of my rope with the ridiculousness of it all. Valuable fresh water was being used to flush the leaky toilet, which was absurd when you considered where you were. Someone had carelessly left a valve open and depleted our entire freshwater supply. I was mad. Now I would have to get a bucket of salt water every time I needed to use the head. And there would be no hot shower after a long, cold day on deck. Tim worked on the machine that makes fresh from salt water until I went to bed. It seemed hopeless. But I resolved to overcome my anger and frustration. I couldn't blow a gasket. Arch was out of epoxy. Hadn't I spent the first eight years of my fishing career showering with a deck hose and pooping in a bucket? Yes, I had. I could do it again. And if the captain doesn't complain, nobody complains.

When Archie woke me the next morning, he coolly reported that Tim had fixed the water maker and that he had two of the three computers running again. They must have been up most of the night. I sat in the captain's chair, watched the sun rise, and knew that the worst was behind us. There was virtually nothing left to go wrong. Our teamwork had paid off.

Arch delivered a steaming cup of coffee and said that he would wake the crew when he had breakfast ready. "By the way," Arch said as he started down the stairs, "I think we should do some safety drills soon. I put together a ditch bag to take in the life raft and organized the survival suits to make it easy for everyone to grab one." Although this didn't indicate much confidence in our fine craft, I agreed that drills were in order and thought that perhaps after breakfast would be a good time to start. Safety was one area where bungees and Liquid Skin would not save us. The importance of working together, rather than against one another, is greatest when lives are at risk. Everyone has his own "station" and responsibilities in different types of emergencies. And we all count on everyone else to do his part for the good of the whole. It wouldn't do four of us any good if the fifth couldn't complete his task. What if someone didn't sound the general alarm to alert shipmates of a problem? What if the radioman forgot to call Mayday? What if the guys launched the life raft prematurely? What if someone neglected to bring a survival suit topside for me? What if the EPIRB (the emergency-position-indicating radio beacon) was inadvertently turned off? What if all the vents were not closed in a fire? The what-ifs were endless. There was only one answer— teamwork. Life-threatening situations are the times when a captain most wants to be one of a single, cohesive unit. It certainly would not serve me well to alienate myself from the men I might ultimately count on for my life. But it was a balancing act of sorts, I knew. I had to guard against becoming one of the guys. That was one sure way of losing control of your command. When the time was right to do so, I would make it clear that I was the boss. So far I hadn't needed to.

The smell of bacon made my stomach growl in anticipation. Oh, good, I thought, another low-cal meal. It was no wonder the crew tipped the scales at a good half ton among the four of them. If I wasn't careful, I would leave the boat after two trips shaped just like a porpoise. At my age it was getting difficult to keep my matronly figure. I wasn't vain about most things. But weight had always been an uphill battle. There were five pounds that I'd juggled around on a seasonal rotation, and they had refused to migrate out of belly fat as of late. Maybe if I worked hard this trip, I would at least look a bit fitter than I did right now. I would certainly burn off the rashers of bacon Arch served me. And the eggs and toast. I had been heavier in my younger days of Grand Banks fishing, but in better shape and stronger. Food was always a great diversion. When the chips are down, we eat and forget. I so enjoyed the plate of perfectly cooked eggs that I nearly forgot how rotten the past two days had been. Maybe that really was behind us now.

I was proud of the way we had all pulled together when the going was tough. And I was amazed at my ability to keep my cool. I had grown up, I realized, and out of the childish rages that many a crew had suffered. Ten years ago, in the same sequence of events that I'd endured this trip so far, I would have screamed my voice to extinction. I had never made a full trip without a touch of Grand Banks laryngitis. This would be a first.

It was nearly 10:00 A.M. and time for the daily morning report from the fishing grounds. I hopped out of the chair and reached to turn up the volume on the starboard SSB radio. The digital frequency display indicated that the radio had been set to 2182.0 megahertz, which is the emergency channel. That was curious, I thought as I turned the knob clockwise one click and then back in the other direction two clicks. I distinctly remembered leaving the starboard radio tuned to 3417.0 so that I could eavesdrop on the fleet and better plan my fishing strategy. Or was it the port radio that Timmy had finally succeeded in accidentally tuning to the right frequency? No, it was definitely the starboard. I now scanned a few more turns to the right and then back to the left. There was no three-megahertz channel. I felt the heat rise from the pit of my stomach to my neck and eventually to my face, where it burned. Angst increased with every spin of the knob. Someone had frigged with my radio! I spun the knob wildly, searching for anything that resembled the secret channel. I tried the other knob, which controlled the "groups" of channels in bunches of one hundred. Between the two knobs, I knew that the radio had the capability to store thousands of channels, and this knowledge fed my growing anger.

Playing with electronics while on watch is absolutely forbidden in my book. Plus, this radio wasn't like the one in your car; it had many knobs and buttons and was extremely complex to program. What could have possessed someone to change the frequency of the radio to the emergency channel? This was the breaking of what I considered a cardinal rule. Was someone planning to make a Mayday call? This seeming OCD behavior on my part could really become a question of life or death. I was now turning both knobs at once, one with the right hand and one with the left, both in the same direction, then toward each other and then away in opposite directions. The more I searched, the further I seemed to be getting from where I started. And there seemed to be no hope of returning. The blood that had now left my hands had accumulated in my temples, where it surged faster with every turn of the knobs. I clenched my teeth and resisted the urge to rip the microphone cord from the receiver. It was now 10:15. I wondered what the fish reports had been and whether anyone had given bearings of where they were working. I wondered how many fish had been caught so far today, and in what temperature water, and how deep, and with what type of bait. . . . I wondered how far ahead of us Scotty was, and when he would be making his first set, and where.

Just as I was ready to give up and find a heavy object with which to crush the radio, there it was—3417.0 flashed in the orange-lit digital display. Scotty was just signing off. He thanked Charlie Johnson for the information, wished him luck tonight, and said he would be north of him tomorrow and making his first set. Then the radio went back to static. I had missed the entire report. I let my arms drop to my sides from the radio over my head. My hands tingled. So Scotty would be fishing tomorrow night. I wondered where the small fleet was working and whether I could possibly reach the area by tomorrow or the next day. I didn't want Scotty to get too much of a head start. I couldn't believe that one of my geniuses had touched my radio. Who did they think they were? Watch meant watch; it did not mean play captain with the electronics. I took a deep breath, said to hell with self-control, and stepped out the back door of the wheelhouse.

Archie and Hiltz stood at the fish hold's hatch. Arch was applying a little Liquid Skin to the end of his thumb, while Dave ran a knife over a sharpening stone. They sure looked happy down there in the sun. I was pissed. I started down the ladder and was cursing before my feet hit the deck. In my own defense, I did not lose control. It was a conscious—if spontaneous—decision to go nuts. "Which one of you jerks decided to tune the radio?" They looked at each other, then back at me. "Some fucking idiot changed the frequency from where I had set it, and I just missed the fishing report." This was met with looks of surprise and silence. "There are too many fucking captains aboard here! What the fuck? If anyone dares touch anything in the wheelhouse again . . ." And on and on I went. It was bad. Once I started, I couldn't stop my-self. I swore. I threatened. I belittled. I called them names. I think I may even have stomped my feet.

"How were your eggs?" Arch asked with a tiny smile. That seared me. I wanted Archie to fight back. If anyone had assaulted me verbally, I would have uncorked like shaken champagne. I wanted these men to defend themselves and pledge their innocence or ignorance or something. I wanted them to give me something to take another swipe at. But they simply stood and stared at my face as it deepened in redness. This was Archie's gentle way of telling me everything was okay, and that I should take a deep breath. I took that breath, and the men went back to the knife and the thumb, unscathed.

CHAPTER 7

Let's Catch Fish

S o the jig was up. And, I realized, being captain had a lot in common with love—it meant never having to say "I'm sorry." Thinking back, I couldn't recall ever apologizing to crew for lashing out, or anything else for that matter. I certainly would not begin now, which was significant to me in that it indicated a stoicism of sorts. It was practically tangible proof that I could point to and say with something well nigh to conviction, "There. See, I haven't changed." As strange as this may sound, rather than being embarrassed for my outburst, I was in fact relieved that I still had it in me. And so spontaneous! I wouldn't waste any more time wondering whether my newfound ability to remain cool in any calamity was a result of maturity or a desire to portray myself in any particular way. That point was now moot.

Another pimple of positivity that came to the surface of this irritated boil of a situation was my ability to remain unmoved by what others might see as a blunder on my part. It's a type of grace that a person is born with, I think. It can't be learned. Either you have it or you don't. I've always had a knack for manipulating the sun at the center of my personal universe to keep me in the most favorable light, no matter what degree of cloudiness I have created. An offshoot of this mentality is the fact that it's nearly impossible to embarrass or insult me. Some might call it being thick-skinned. I would disagree. But whatever the case, this psychological twisting of "never let them see you sweat" had served me well through the years. It's not that I do not sweat. I just don't admit that I sweat. That's not to say that I have the power to bend light in the eyes of others. Basically I'm a master of self-deception. The upside of viewing life through rose-colored glasses is a deep and relentless optimism regardless of how bad others sharing a situation might perceive it to be. The downside is real disappointment and frequent disenchantment when reality finds its way through the sparkling glitter of my vision.

Archie and Dave had not been bothered by my tantrum. They had taken it neither personally nor seriously. Although their reaction was never verbalized, I got a sense that they found it humorous. Word spread quickly through the ranks, and the phrase of the week became "Meanwhile, aboard the *Seahawk* . . ." The original trigger point—that I didn't want anyone else playing captain—was lost when the handwritten sign that I posted in the wheelhouse—DO NOT PUSH BUTTONS, TURN KNOBS, OR ADJUST <u>ANYTHING</u>!!!—was replaced with one that Archie designed on his PC and printed in bold red letters. He even included all three exclamation points. There had been times, and this was one of them, when I found it easier to deal with fish than with fishermen. It was most definitely time to get fishing. Then the crew and I would all unite against a common enemy—the sword.

Swordfish and I had been adversaries for a long time, I thought as I sat back in the chair and mused over the bow and into the future. I like to think that I know my enemy, and reflecting on the past would be most helpful in reacquainting myself with this one. I had read most of the small amount of literature available on the biology of swordfish, and some of it is contradictory, indicating how little is actually known. Personal experience and observations through the course of my twenty-year work-study had taught me most of what I know about the behavior of swordfish. I couldn't help speculating on what that same experience had taught the fish. There have always been fish that just can't be outsmarted. And that is critical to their ultimate survival. I wondered what swordfish know about this predator and was immediately embarrassed by the thought. Did the fish know I no longer had a *need* to catch them? Did they know that wants were as strong as needs in me? Did they realize the lengths to which I would go to fulfill this particular want? What I wanted most in the world at this moment was to put a slammer trip of fish aboard the *Seahawk*. The fulfillment of this deep-seated desire hinged on my ability to know my enemy to the point of knowing where they would be prior to their arrival.

When I say "I love swordfish," I am not necessarily commenting on them as a meal, although I surely do enjoy them in that capacity. Swordfish are the most interesting creatures! They are fascinating and intriguing in their unique combination of fish and sword—like a unicorn, but real. The facts and figures surrounding swordfish perhaps explain what makes them so worthy of my lifetime pursuit of them. The speed at which they travel, the distances they cover in their migration, and their strength all contribute to the quality most frequently attributed to them, elusiveness. I can't imagine a life spent digging clams or trapping slime eels—they're just so . . . ordinary. What's to know about a clam? You traipse around the clam flats looking for holes in the surface of the mud. One hole, one clam, as my Aunt Gracie used to say. You see a hole, you dig, and you find a clam. Big deal. A clam does not possess the ability to dodge the digger. Swordfish, in contrast, are mysterious and challenging and sexy. You never hear stories about the giant clam that got away. Clams have no personality. You've seen one clam, you've seen them all.

Although I had never regarded swordfish merely as hunks of meat, I sensed that my feelings about my relationship with the fish had grown into something more intimate or substantial in the past ten years when I was not pursuing them. Was this an example of absence making the heart grow fonder? No, nothing so sentimental. Time is money. I had a lot invested in this relationship. Defining that relationship is more complex (for "complex," read "confusing") than doing the same for most of my others. Each individual swordfish is an entity to be reckoned with. Long-lining is not casting a net and hauling in whatever gets in the way. It's a plan of attack that targets fish one at a time. Patterns of behavior lead to numbers being caught. But still, there is a point in each fish's capture or release when it's a one-on-one fight. That's the romantic part. The most beautiful and stoic picture in the fishery is the image of one human finessing one fish. Until the fish is either dead on the deck or swimming away, that relationship is absolutely tentative. The flip of a tail could amount to slack line and sunken hearts aboard the boat. The wrap of a line around something too solid results in the same line going slack. Weary arms and impatience also lead to pulled hooks and lost fish. Heavy weather always plays on the side of the sword. Often, big tangles of gear come aboard devoid of a fish that must have escaped before the real match. At times it seems that fish have a huge advantage in the battle.

Do fish have the capacity to experience feelings of defeat or triumph? The belief that they do makes catching them that much more intense an experience. Who wants to engage in battle with a rock? I have in the past maintained that anthropomorphism is Greek to me. But it's impossible to avoid attributing human characteristics, motivations, and qualities to a swordfish once you've encountered one eye to eye in its last gasp before succumbing, or once you've sensed the bravado in the slap of a tail of one fresh off the hook and diving for freedom. It's an egotistical world that I live in. It's a world that revolves around all I know and believe. Swordfish, among everything else, can be described and understood only in terms of "me." Once I discovered that swordfish are monogamous, I perceived the partners of those dead on hooks I'd hauled that followed their mates to the surface, allowing me to harpoon them, as suicidal. We call them "twofers" and believe that the survivor of the hook just could not go on without its better half. We, according to our own lore, put the second fish out of its misery. As ridiculous as that sounds, if you haven't been there, you haven't been there.

On the other end of the sword personality spectrum is the fish as a warrior. *Xiphias gladius* is the Braveheart of the ocean. With few existing natural predators, swordfish through the ages have probably wiped out anything that could have been a threat. Their flat, double-edged bill is a built-in weapon. And nothing wields a weapon more quickly or with more dexterity than a swordfish. I have seen their samurai act firsthand. I now remembered that episode with the same amazement I'd felt when seeing the original version.

It was way back in my college days when I worked the deck of the *Walter Leeman* for Alden Leeman during summer breaks. We fished Georges Bank this particular trip, and because of that we were able to long-line and harpoon. You see, Georges is one of the few places in the world where swordfish "fin," or come to the surface, making them targets for "stick fishing." It was a blistering-hot day, the type that almost never occurs offshore. We had hauled aboard the last of the longline gear and jogged up onto the bank to look for finners. The water was cooler up on the shoals, creating a low layer of wispy fog that curled and drifted aimlessly over the surface like steam on a hot skillet. Harpooning was my favorite part of any day, and I scrambled up to the crow's nest, where I took my newly won position of helmsman. I had eyes that could literally see fish, plain and simple. I could see them far away. I could see them close by. And I could see them underwater and anticipate where they would break the surface next. I could see fish that others could not, no matter how vigorously I pointed or directed by hour of the clock or compass rose. There was a method to my scan, and it worked. Although five of us looked, I spotted 90 percent of the fish we successfully "ironed" that season.

As soon as I was situated at the top of the mast, Alden switched the engine controls from the wheelhouse to where I could drive, with the aim of putting the boat on any fish I could find so that Alden could throw the dart. There was only one way to put the boat on a fish. That was to lead the fish with the bow of the boat, or to sort of maneuver the boat so that our paths intersected stem to sword in a crossing fashion. Not head-on or by the tail, as either of those approaches would spook the fish before it was close enough to attempt a throw of the harpoon. The fish doesn't get nervous as long as it has an eye on what's coming. That alone speaks volumes about swordfish attitude. A seventy-foot vessel powered by a six-hundred-horse diesel engine, looming high above the surface as well as cutting through well below, does not cause a fish to make a quick exit unless it comes from behind. I was well versed in boat handling, and I learned the strategy quickly under Alden's tutelage. We, as a team, had been quite formidable. Of course, we owed a lot of our prowess to Alden's ability to really pitch the pole, launching a Hail Mary shot and making miraculous contact.

My hands were black with soot from the exhaust that coated the mast and the rungs of the ladder I scaled to achieve the highest post on the boat. From below, Alden shouted an occasional compass heading for me to follow as we poked along hoping for fins. I searched the horizon—all 360 degrees of it—which was relatively close in the hazy conditions. On every other rotation, I looked down, deep into the water all around the boat. The rest of the crew was just coming out of the fish hold, where they had iced what the hooks had produced today. They yelled up that they were going to the galley for lunch and would bring me a sandwich when they came up the mast to help look. It was almost getting to be a joke. I knew they wouldn't see anything. They knew it, too. "Come on, Linda! Find us a fish!" And they disappeared like ants into a hill beneath me. Some days Alden would let the crew nap while we harpooned, waking them only to haul the rigs back aboard and take care of the fish. But this hadn't been the best day hookwise, and Alden wasn't in the most charitable mood. So after lunch it would be all hands in the mast or on the forward deck.

I wanted badly to find a fish before the rest of the crew emerged from the fo'c'sle, which I suppose is some weird fallout from my competitive nature. Or perhaps it's due to selfishness. Being alone in the crow's nest and driving the boat onto a fish to be stuck with a hand-thrown harpoon is the most exciting and exhilarating experience. It's a thrill that is addictive, and there was a desire in me to not water it down with company. It all starts with fins cutting the surface. The dart penetrates fish. The line zips overboard, ripped from clothespins that hold it along the pulpit—*snap, snap, snap*—I can still feel that sound. I looked hard, with the belief that if you search hard enough, you can produce fish. Working in the crow's nest is also my deepest connection to the past. Harpooning is the most primitive and fundamental way to catch a fish. It's a frenzied sensation that I suspect I must share with the whalers of old.

As I was scanning the horizon over the port bow, a splash caught my eye off to the starboard. I concentrated on where the surface was riled up, thinking it could have been a porpoise or a tuna, as swordfish rarely breach. Fins cut the surface and then disappeared. It was too quick for me to identify as a sword. My heart raced as I pushed the throttle up and turned toward where I had seen the fins, hoping for another look. There they were again! They were big and wide-set. It must be a great fish, I thought, as Alden made his way out to the end of the pulpit and untied the harpoon. A second pair of fins popped out, seemingly chasing the first. They were different, and I recognized them as shark fins. Too stiff for blue shark. When they broke the surface again, we were closer. "Mako!" I yelled, and prayed we would beat the shark to the fish, as I knew that the shortfin mako is one of the swordfish's only natural predators. The water roiled as the two sets of fins clashed and then submerged. I slowed the boat and kept looking at the spot where the fish had been.

"Can you still see them?" Alden shouted from the stand.

"Yes. I can see shadows, but they're too deep to hit. It looks like the sword is attacking the shark!" And back to the surface they came, all thrashing and throwing water about. They were close off our starboard side. They separated and stayed on the surface, circling each other like dueling gunfighters preparing to draw. From my vantage point, I could see a cloud of blood in the water. Alden instructed me to put him on the mako first, since he knew that the fish would surely be eaten by the shark once it was disadvantaged by the harpoon. I was full of nervous excitement. I'd seen fish and sharks tangle before, but always when the fish had been in the vulnerable situation of being stuck on a hook and tethered to longline gear. I'd seen on too many occasions the remains of what a mako shark can't eat before we haul it away and aboard the boat. The fish never fares well. But this mako was going after a free swimmer!

As we neared, the mako was swimming directly behind the swordfish, as if it would take a bite out of its tail. My heart raced faster as I estimated the sword to weigh at least three hundred pounds, which would be a day saver. And the mako looked even bigger. We had to kill the shark before it got the fish! Suddenly the swordfish turned 180 degrees—in the length of its body—and slashed at the shark with its massive bill. More blood streamed. Alden turned to his right and launched the harpoon. He ironed the mako dead in the center of its fins—"backboning," as we say when the spine is severed, killing the fish instantly. The shark sank, pulling the dart line from the boat slowly until the buoy marking the end went over the side.

I put the boat in gear and made a lazy circle around the buoy. I searched the water around the boat for the swordfish. I scanned the horizon. I looked deep. There were no fins. There was no cigar-shaped purple shadow below. I prayed that the fish would give us a shot. Alden had rerigged the harpoon with another dart and line, then waited poised to throw at the end of the narrow stand sticking out from the bow much like the bill from a fish. "Where's the sword?" Alden asked, without looking up.

"I don't see it," I answered, without looking at him.

"Jesus Christ! Did you take your eyes off the fish? It was a monster!" Alden was pissed. I was disappointed, and I knew from experience not to remind the captain that he had ordered me to go onto the shark first. I kept looking, but the fish was gone. Alden kept crabbing at me about losing the fish. He blamed me. I was used to it. Besides, I realized that if I took some credit for the fish we got, I also had to shoulder some of the responsibility for the ones that got away. The more Alden bitched, the more I started resenting the swordfish for tricking us. We had been lured into a ploy to kill the sword's worst enemy. I felt like a character in one of Aesop's fables, where the animals teach some moral lesson. But I didn't know what the lesson was.

It was a frustrating afternoon, with only one buoy bobbing around to show for our effort. When it came time to think about setting the longline, Alden had one of the guys haul the rig with the mako attached. The shark came aboard all limp, as we expected. It had deep gashes and long cuts from its fight with the sword. We all agreed that this was indeed a first, to see a mako lose a battle with a swordfish. This swordfish, the one that got away, was the warrior of all warriors. The crew was skeptical about the details I supplied. I guess I wouldn't have believed the story either if I hadn't seen it myself. When the butcher cleaned the shark and examined the contents of its stomach, he exclaimed with some amazement about a small fish he found among the half-digested foodstuff in the shark's recent diet. I inspected the fish along with the rest of the crew. It was the tiniest baby sword any of us had ever seen. We surmised the one that got away to have been the baby's mother, and I felt better about her escape and no longer resented her for tricking me into killing the shark.

That was my first memory of actually attributing human emotion and motivation to a fish. It's a foolish exercise. But it helps make sense of things I can't otherwise understand. And I take comfort in knowing that the inclination to twist, justify, and reason the unreasonable is somewhat universal. Thinking about it now as I steamed along, I had to admit that I'd been outsmarted by many fish. I'll never learn the answer to what cerebral abilities and emotional capacities fish have. But believing that they're more than just hunks of meat makes my life considerably more interesting. Respect for the intellect of fish, beyond thinking that they are merely eating and reproducing machines, levels the playing field, in my mind, and eases the pain of unfair accusations of slaughtering innocent fish.

I nearly laughed out loud when I realized the thought process in which I'd just indulged myself. I had proven, beyond the shadow of a doubt, that the cumulative effect of age on one's mind is overwhelming. My crew would've laughed me out of the wheelhouse if they could read my thoughts, including all this drivel about fish

psyche. I wondered how Alden *really* felt about fish. Was his relationship to them one-dimensional? Was his mentality one that
could only handle killing something he regarded as inanimate?
Killer instinct tarnishes with age. It's there, just different from
what it was in youth.

I would make better use of my thinking time by concentrating
on a harder science than what others would regard as the soft—
fish psychology. As far as I was concerned, all science surrounding
swordfish is brittle. There are a few undeniable truths about the
swordfish that make its capture possible, or at least more likely
than not. Unlike me, swordfish are cold-blooded predators. They
do have feeding routines and habits. The longline is designed to
maximize and take advantage of known fish habits and tendencies.
For example, swordfish feed daily, usually at night when they rise
to the surface to chase pelagic bait fish. They seem to bite better on
the nights surrounding the full moon. Thus our daily loop of set
and haul, with maximum soak time to accommodate the nocturnal feeders, syncing our trips with the lunar cycle. Swordfish do
not travel in schools. Loners or loose aggregations are the norm.
Therefore long-lining and harpooning are the preferred and proven
methods of fishing for them. They feed on bait that congregates on
the current changes where two bodies of water meet. For example,
where the Gulf Stream and the Labrador Current come together is
ideal. Swordfish are highly migratory; this pattern dictates the sea-
sonality. There's no sense fishing the Grand Banks in the winter.
Their sense of sight is keen. Therefore we make use of visual aids
on our gear, like light sticks and spinners and glowing beads that
might attract fish. Swordfish have the ability to physically heat
their eyes and brain when surfacing from the depths, increasing

their vision. They have some sense of smell, making the use of cod liver oil helpful in luring them to hooks. They may even have some degree of hearing. We sometimes use rattles on leaders. Swordfish are powerful swimmers. So the snaps that attach leaders to the main line are designed to slide, and not jam when a fish realizes it's hooked. Great bait and sharp hooks are the most basic keys to success once the gear is in the water. Swords are a spawn fish. Females carry over 1 million eggs, allowing swordfish to remain strong as a species while being harvested one at a time by hooks. Swordfish are quite adept at feeding themselves, and there's not much hope of outsmarting them. So fishermen basically have to drop the hooks on their heads in order to have any degree of success. Be in the right location. Serve something appetizing. Rig proper gear.

It was disconcerting to register so little on my swordfish fact sheet after nearly twenty years of intense study. I thought I knew my adversary. Perhaps some of my past success stemmed from my solid trust in the fact that I don't *really* know anything about catching fish. At least not compared with men who fish on species that are a more cooperative study subject. Some types of fish just lend themselves better to the microscope than swordfish do. The realization that I know so little has fed my desire to work harder to compensate for my lack of knowledge. Covering all the bases every night and avoiding putting all eggs in a single basket were hard-learned lessons. Every time I believed I had swordfish figured out, they threw me a curve. They're clever, and elusive, and mysterious. Swordfish and I first engaged in this game of hide-and-seek in 1979. And thirty years later we're both still in the game. These realizations led me to a grudging respect for swordfish. I do admire their tenacity. This game is a dance of sorts, or a collaboration. We, the fish and I, both have our jobs to do. Any given day it's a toss-up which of us is doing our job better. Sometimes I feel like a gallant saltwater cowboy busting broncos. Other times I just wait for my horse to be shot out from under me. Damn fish. I laughed to myself. Our relationship is weirder than any I'd had with humans of the opposite sex. And I'd had some weird ones.

As we plodded our way merrily to the east, I had nearly resigned myself to the fact that Scotty would reach the fishing grounds far enough in advance of us that he'd get in a night, or possibly two, before we set a hook. Chompers on the *Bigeye* might be leaving Newfoundland soon, and there were a handful of other boats stretching out gear where I would like to be, including a couple of big producers from Nova Scotia. That was just the way it was. And there wasn't a thing I could do to change it. I did hold on to the hope that Mother Nature would do me a favor (not that one was owed) by kicking up a major disturbance that would keep the others from fishing but not slow *our* progress toward the grounds. All I asked was a small, intense, localized gale directly on top of the *Eagle Eye II*. Nothing dangerous, but bad enough to cause Scotty to sit and wait while I caught up would be optimum. Even a little gale-force wind could stir the sea to a state that could prohibit the transfer of Scotty's crew from boat to boat. And no crew would mean no fishing, I thought gleefully. Perhaps Chompers would run into complications ashore that would delay his departure. As the next forty-eight hours passed, it became clear that weather would not be a factor east of the Grand Banks, where the boats were enjoying decent fishing and beautiful conditions.

As the buzz on the radio indicated Scotty's nearness to his first set, we approached the west side of the Grand Banks. It was about noon when I realized that we had a shot at setting gear that night. It was not uncommon to find a puddle of warm water pushed up onto the west side of the bank, where the depth of water shoaled abruptly. And the right temperature water "on soundings" could produce some very healthy swordfish, I knew. I inspected the chart and chose a waypoint to steam to. Jukes Canyon was a place that I remembered from the past as a possibility. Although I'd never had great success on the west side, others had. There was always plenty of motivation and rationale to fish the west side, rather than steaming the extra distance across the bank and way off to the east. Time and fuel were both burning incentives, not to mention my competitive nature, which fanned the flames. I kept fingers crossed as we closed the gap between "not tonight" and "maybe."

The guys assured me that we were in great shape with regard to gear. They had accomplished the building of twelve hundred leaders in their spare minutes between emergency repairs and were as excited as I was at the possibility of getting the real show started. As with any job, most of the work is in the preparation. Like house-painters dipping the brush into a freshly opened can of paint after days of scraping, sanding, and taping, we were closing in on the part that made the difference. When we had reached the thousand-fathom curve, I had convinced myself that we would set gear tonight unless the water temperature was ridiculously sharky.

Cold water could really produce sharks. But it is also where the slammer swords lurk. A few blue sharks didn't scare me, so long as the odd swordfish came along with them. Blue sharks were a nuisance that needed to be handled in some number when you were fishing the Grand Banks of Newfoundland regardless of water temperature. But it always seemed that the greatest sharking-ups were a result of the cold side of the temperature gradients we traditionally fished. And the danger in sharks went beyond their fearsome teeth. Sharks chew up expensive gear and valuable, limited time. Twelve hundred brand-new leaders . . . Still fresh in my mind was advice from shoreside captains about fishing colder than I had in the past. Everyone had shifted to the cool side, they said, as it was where the fatter, healthier fish were coming from. I recalled hearing that John Caldwell, the captain of the *Eagle Eye II* before Scotty, had fished water as cold as fifty-six degrees his last trip. I never used to fish water that cool. But in the ten years that I was off the water, the use of circle hooks had been mandated by law, and mackerel was the bait of choice. That combination apparently worked well in the cold water.

When I found sixty-two-degree water inside five hundred fathoms, my pulse quickened in anticipation of what I knew was a very good sign. Bait fish often linger around depth changes—or bottom contour, as seen on a navigational chart. And when water the right temperature pushes over relatively shallow depths, it can mean big fishing.

I jogged the *Seahawk* to a position at the head of Jukes Canyon and very close to Canada's two-hundred-mile limit. When setting gear this close to the boundary line, it is imperative to ensure that your gear will drift away from the line, farther out to sea and therefore deeper into the international zone fished by every country with a fleet. Unless you're a Canadian citizen, you are not welcome to fish north of the boundary line that encompasses the water out to two hundred miles from the shores of Newfoundland. Canada patrols the line vigilantly with boats and airplanes, protecting her water from poachers.

I knocked the engine out of gear in order to perform a "drift test." I had always done drift tests in the past, regardless of my proximity to any boundaries, to check the speed and direction of the current in which I was preparing to set gear. I usually had the best luck fishing the faster-moving water on the edge of the Gulf Stream. As a general rule, the areas that Grand Bankers like most are where the stream meets the slower-moving, colder Labrador Current. Places where these two bodies of water collide most dramatically produce sharp temperature breaks, or gradients, that are relatively easy to follow. The most common practice when fishing a break is to weave the forty-mile line back and forth across the different temperatures that signify a current change. Current changes, or tide breaks or rips, naturally collect critters low in the food chain, which is why they are so productive. As Ringo would say, "Where there's prey, there's a predator."

The wind was light and variable, so it had little or no effect on our drift. I pushed a button on the plotter, leaving an event mark on the screen to represent our present position, and went below to check the deck and take a "down temp" reading. The gauge in the wheelhouse used to find and follow breaks measures the temperature close to the surface, as its transducer is in a through-hull fitting. The sending unit is no deeper than wherever it is fixed through the hull, in this case probably eight feet. And our gear was rigged to fish at a depth of about ten fathoms. So if there was ice water at ten fathoms, or sixty feet, below a warmer surface, I would be stupid to fish here. I had a need to know the temperature at sixty feet.

Some boats have towable temperature sensors, or "down

temps," fixed to a fin that swims at a depth the captain specifies. These are towed almost constantly and really make a difference, in that the captain knows the water temperature at the depth he is fishing, in addition to what's going on at the surface. If the hooks are dangling at a depth of ten fathoms below the surface, it's helpful to know the temperature there. But the *Seahawk* was not so equipped. Instead we had a jury-rigged sensor, duct-taped to a lead window-sash weight, attached to an electrical extension cord that was wired into a digital readout mounted inside a small Plexiglas window that could only be seen from where I would stand to haul the gear back. Our rig could not be towed. So lying to with the boat out of gear while conducting a drift test was a good opportunity to take a down temp. Because ours could not be towed while steaming, spot checks were the only option. "This is better than nothing," I said as Arch assisted me in untangling loops of electrical cord that had been stored in a plastic milk crate.

"Not really," Arch replied when he peeked at the gauge after paying overboard ten fathoms of cord. "Unless the water temperature is seventy-seven degrees down there, I'd say this thing is junk."

I squeezed myself into a spot where I could also see the readout. The red digital numbers jumped up and down in thirty-degree skips. "That isn't very helpful," I said with a slight chuckle. "The temperature is somewhere between fifty and seventy. I knew that without the gauge."

"I guess I'm not surprised that it doesn't work. I'll see if I can fix it," Arch said. "What does the gauge in the wheelhouse say?"

"I bumped her out of gear in sixty-five. The color of the water is good," I said as I leaned over the rail and stared into the blue abyss. There is a certain color and clarity, almost like a visual texture, to water that produces the most fish and the fewest sharks. I tried to bring those qualities to the surface from the depth of ten years. "I think this looks fine."

"We gonna try it?"

"As long as the current isn't doing anything funky, we'll start setting at four-thirty," I said as I headed back to the bridge. When I entered the wheelhouse I was happy to see that the surface temperature had risen slightly: up to 66.1 from 65.2, where I had begun the drift test. I looked at the plotter and could see that we had drifted a short distance to the southeast from the event mark. Perfect, I thought. The GPS indicated that we were moving at 1.4 knots and 147 degrees. This was ideal. If I set the gear around the head of Jukes Canyon and it drifted in a southerly direction, the string of gear would pull down and through the canyon and fish a variety of depths through the night. Sharp depth changes, like tide breaks, are places where feed is abundant. And Jukes Canyon had fairly steep walls on either side. With the current at this pace and direction, if I made a good set, one-third of the gear would drift from shallow to deep, another third would drift from deep to shallow, and the middle third would move through the center of the canyon. Birds worked the surface of the water as far as I could see. I couldn't have ordered a better situation. I yelled below for the guys to get bait out of the freezer for eight hundred hooks.

Happy . . . perfect . . . ideal . . . I hoped I wasn't kidding myself. I knew better than to get overzealous. But I couldn't help it. This is what we had come for. This is what I do. And, to my mind, things looked good.

CHAPTER 8

Setting Out, at Last

I was feeling extremely anxious to get the gear set out, but I knew well the hazards of putting the gear into the water too early. If the gear moves through the fish before "the bite," or feeding time, you stand a good chance of missing them altogether. The peak of the moon, or when it reaches its highest and brightest point in each twenty-four-hour cycle, is an hour later every night. Bait fish come to the surface in the light of the moon. Thus swordfish feed relatively close to the surface at night while chasing bait fish, and so the peak of the swordfish bite is an hour later each night, beginning at the first trace of a moon. This far after the full moon, it would be wise to be patient and set a bit later than when the moon was at its first-quarter phase, so that the hooks didn't drift out of where they were set before the bite. Until very recent years, most of us believed that swordfish were nocturnal feeders, eating exclusively at night. But savvy sports fishermen off the coast of Florida had proved otherwise. If you can get a hook to bottom in water deeper than a mile, you can catch fish during the day. That is pretty tricky but doable with a couple of hooks and an electric reel. Not an option here and now, though. We were Grand Banks commercial long-liners. Patience not being a personal virtue, I found it hard to wait.

Of course I was aware that it was possible to set too late. Again, the string of gear needs to be in the water during the bite. And the longer the gear is in the water, the more distance it covers by drifting. Distance covered with movement in the current is advantageous when you're fishing just a temperature break. But it's not so good when fishing a depth change, as the gear will be out of the catching zone as soon as it moves away from soundings. The sun was still directly overhead, and there was not yet any sign of a moon. I forced myself to wait.

I made the most of the waiting by scoping out the water temperature in the area and planning what I imagined would be a thirty-mile set of eight hundred hooks. I would start offshore, or south of the bank itself, in deeper water, follow the west edge of Jukes to the north until I was close to the Canadian line, then turn around the head of the canyon and back offshore along the east edge. The set would be a rough horseshoe with both ends offshore. Knowing that the bend in the middle of the gear would drift offshore, or into deeper water, I wanted to get that part as shoal, or shallow, as I could. When I reached the spot where I wanted to start, I did another drift test that showed the same direction and speed of the current. A knot and a half isn't a lot of tide, not like out to the east, where we often fish in three knots.

But this current was plenty fast enough to move the gear through a range of depths to cover all the bases in this first set. With any luck we would get a good enough sign of fish on some part of the gear to merit staying right here and fine-tuning.

Most successful trips in my experience were not put together with a few miracle sets. Good trips were more of a grinding away at okay fishing and maximizing opportunity with every set made. Anyone can get lucky and land on a pile of fish once. The real trick is staying on them. Paying attention and tweaking a set had always been my specialty. I could grind with the best of them. Making the best set possible each and every night, and not allowing effort or attention to lapse, was how we would put our trip aboard. We would make as many sets as we needed, based on our daily average. If the fishing was slow, we would fish more nights. Focus is the key. Like a dog with a bone, I could gnaw away relentlessly.

A captain I fished with many years ago, Alan Whipple, would not approve of my decision to go with less than the entire spool of line. Whipple always set every inch of line and every available hook, regardless of weather or any other deterrent. I had learned that from him, and normally I followed it. But I had some reservations about getting in over my head with the very first set aboard the *Seahawk*. We were still in the shakedown process. Things could go very wrong. Eight hundred hooks over the course of thirty miles was a respectable amount of gear. If some critical piece of the puzzle failed to snap in—like the hydraulic motor that drives the main spool—thirty miles would be too much gear. To set less would be wimpy. And too short a string wouldn't show me anything about what was here for fish. There were many reasons that justified setting less than the full string, including my question about ability—the boat's, the crew's, and mine. This hairline crack in my confidence was another reason to make our first set here, rather than diving in among the fleet to the east. A much younger me would have done a careless cannonball right in the middle of the fleet and not worried about any adverse aftershock. I had definitely developed a more thorough thought process in the last ten years, I realized. I was actually being considerate.

The worst situation I could imagine would be to have forty miles of gear wedged between two other boats and not be able to retrieve it. If we suffered some mechanical problem, or if the crew just couldn't get their act together, or if I'd lost the ability to haul, or if I found the adjustment to the port side difficult . . . If we were fishing with the fleet, the inability to do so efficiently would create problems for our neighbors. Gear drifting at three knots ends up in someone else's berth in a short time. That pisses people off. If we couldn't get the gear out and back in a timely manner, I would prefer that to happen with no witnesses. Yet another reason to work the bugs out here. No more heedless action on my part. I felt smart.

As the bottom edge of the sun touched the western horizon, I could hardly stand it. I was all worked up to execute the most important part of my job: putting the gear on the fish. Here was something that I had full control of. The boat was precisely where I had determined to be the ideal latitude, longitude, depth, and temperature to begin the set. I stepped out the back door to signal the men to drop the first beeper buoy into our wake. The buoy with the frequency of 1735 had the strongest signal after all our work, so it was designated "end buoy." A beeper would be snapped to the main line at intervals of about three miles, in a sequence according to the list I had made once all the buoys had been tested on deck. I gave Tim a wave. He held a finger in the air, indicating that I had to wait. I couldn't see into the setting house from the bridge, except for through the small hole through which the main line runs from the drum, over the setting table, and over the transom. I could see Hiltz standing holding a hook baited with a mackerel, ready to toss. And Arch was in the middle of the deck, pulling thawed bait out of water and into plastic boxes. We were apparently waiting for Machado.

Former crew members had learned the hard way to not make me wait when I'm ready to set the gear. I fought the urge to yell to throw the buoy and ask how many men they thought they needed to get started. I waited. This would never have happened aboard the *Hannah Boden*. When I captained her and I was ready to set, I waved and the buoy was dropped. Often my men had waited in the stern for hours ready for the wave, while I steamed around finding the perfect point. I reminded myself that this was not the *Hannah Boden* and silently cursed Machado as we drifted off my start point. I jogged in a lazy circle and back to where I waved to Tim again. This time Tim wasn't looking. He still appeared to be waiting for Machado. We really didn't need four men on deck to set out. In fact, the job can be done with two experienced guys if the boat goes slowly enough. But Machado was the only one with real longline experience. I guessed the other men felt they needed him to get going. I waited a little longer.

By the time Machado sauntered down the deck, I was agitated. But I saw no value in reaming him out. If he was going to be my deck boss, I would not reprimand him in front of the rest of the crew. Organizationally, commercial fishing vessels are strange and interesting entities. Crew dynamics are nothing short of . . . well, dynamic. By no means a democracy, a fishing boat is closer to a dictatorship, and the captain's word is usually law. There is often a certain amount of undercurrent among the crew, but this remains among the crew. A first mate or deck boss emerges from the ranks and is seldom successfully appointed by the captain. A certain pecking order forms, usually stacking up on top of the greenhorn who assumes most of the jobs nobody else wants. Engineer is a title. But that's about it. Keeping things going in the engine room is a thankless job. The cook, although it's not the most coveted position because of the frustration involved in preparing an edible meal in heavy weather, does have fringe benefits. The cook procures the groceries or grub for the trip, so he never runs out of his own favorite soft drink or cereal. The cook also has more opportunity than his shipmates to leave the deck in order to "thaw the roast" or "preheat the oven," and he usually returns to work in the elements looking dryer than when he left and smoking a fresh cigarette. Right now I was glad that Machado was not our cook, as his present mode of operation indicated that he might really milk the job of galley slave.

Machado further annoyed me when he stopped, halfway to his work site, to pull on his gloves. This was a painful process. It seemed to take him forever to get his fingers wiggled in and arranged just right. If Machado was to lead the charge on deck, it wouldn't be much of a strike. I was feeling sick to my stomach with anxiety when he finally waddled around the corner and out of my sight, taking his position, I assumed, at the other side of the setting table across from Hiltz. Once they all got their feet under them and comfortable with the process and routine, I knew that one of the other guys would take control of the deck.

I waved with the hope that the third time would indeed be the charm. Tim nodded and dropped 1735 off our starboard aft quarter and into the water. As we steamed away from the buoy, the drum began to turn, unwinding as line was pulled off and into the wake. Dave and Machado stood on either side of the line in the stern. They baited hooks, tossed them into the water, and clipped snaps to the line. After three leaders went out, Timmy snapped on a float. Three hooks, then a float; three hooks, then a float; over and over until the end of a three-mile section was marked with the next beeper. We were fishing!

As the men worked the stern, I stood and stared at the depth and temperature gauges, turning the boat slightly one way, then the other, to maximize both. About ten minutes into the five-hour setting process, I noticed that I hadn't heard the first beeper, 1735, transmit since it hit the water. I knew that it had functioned properly on deck, because we'd tested it several times. I turned up the volume on the RDF (radio direction finder) and waited for the buoy to transmit. Nothing. No surprise. But I had intended to steam back to 1735 tonight and haul the gear from that end in the morning. Oh, well, a change of plans was okay. I turned up the volume on the two-way loudspeaker and told the men to put the snaps on backward to accommodate pulling them off the main line when hauling from the other direction, and I hoped that the other beepers would work. We would lay on the last beeper set and begin hauling there in the morning. If we'd been setting with the fleet to the east, this would not have been an option. When you fish fast-moving water, the gear must be set into the tide and hauled into the tide. Doing the opposite would result in the equivalent of a trip to the Azores in ground lost by not stemming the current constantly. Again, I was relieved to be getting the bugs out here.

An hour into the set, I was totally immersed in my job and loving it. The head work that goes into setting gear had pushed Machado's lackluster attitude from my mind. This had to be the finest example of "getting back on the bike" I'd ever experienced. It was like I had never left the *Hannah Boden*. All the familiar moves and thoughts and anxieties came back without the slightest hint of hesitation. For the captain, there is absolutely nothing physical about setting out. Except for the need to turn an occasional knob, it was all cerebral. Yet I worked so hard at every set I'd ever made that I knew no greater exhaustion. Unlike most longline captains, I make it a policy never to sit down while setting out. By the end of the trip, I would be so tired I would fear falling asleep standing up. This feels good, though. Anticipation for what we would catch grew with every hook that splashed behind the boat.

Fishing is all about putting the hooks in the water. Catching fish is all about putting hooks in the right water. The ability to do so, in my case, was learned mostly through mistakes. I had graduated with honors from the school of hard knocks. I imagine there are a few fishing virtuosos who are born with some innate ability. But for most of us, it's just plain hard work, and it's doing it over and over again. Fishing acumen is a combination of experience and common sense. And in my mind both of these are acquired traits. My skill level increased with age and experience. After twenty years in blue water—even with ten off—I should be damn good. Sure, I would love to have the technological advantages that the other captains in the fleet enjoy. But I had experience, plenty of it.

I had always been very respectful of science and electronics and never considered good production a result of any "feel" for fishing or God-given ability. Most of the boats in the U.S. longline fleet were equipped with computer software that captures satellite imagery to locate fish. This particular program, which wasn't able to be fixed aboard the *Seahawk* before we left the dock, was capable of pinpointing thermal fronts, plankton concentrations, surface eddies, and current speed and directions and overlaying them all on a bathymetric chart. Must be nice, I thought as I watched the depth sounder and surface-temperature gauge. This was the old-school method. Although it had been ten years, the electronic equipment I'd had at my disposal when I left swordfishing was far more sophisticated than the very bare minimums I now focused on. I made up for lack of talent with my stubborn work ethic and by surrounding myself with great equipment and crew. When I returned to make this trip, my intention had not been to go back to an era that preceded my time. I'd thought of it as forward progress. But the drum was spinning, and hooks were being baited. It's fairly basic. I was setting longline gear, and it felt good.

There was some chatter on the radio from the fleet to the east. Scotty had collected his crew from the boat that had delivered them from Newfoundland, and he'd managed to wriggle into the corner of the main break, the most coveted of all fishing spots. There were six boats working the edge, all lined up end to end and jockeying for position in the usual Grand Banks fashion. I hoped

I wouldn't have to join them. If this set could produce enough to keep us here and out of the fray, I would be looking pretty smart for stopping and trying the east side. If we bombed here, I would continue along as if I hadn't stopped, and no one would be the wiser. I hadn't spoken with anyone on the radio lately and realized that none of the other captains were paying attention to my whereabouts. I would remain quiet in hopes of excellent fishing away from the crowd. The jockeying for position among a fleet of hard drivers is a game unto itself. I was good at that game, but everyone always prefers to avoid rush-hour traffic when possible. I wouldn't have to fight to hold my ground here. There was nobody to fight with.

As I turned the corner and headed south-southeast along the east side of the canyon, the depth sounder began to light up with brilliant-colored blobs suspended in the black background of the screen. This lava-lamp look was something to get excited about. I knew that the dark-colored, misshapen forms were tight schools of bait following krill rising from the ocean floor. Bait, usually small squid, capelin, or ballyhoo, feed on clouds of krill, which are like tiny shrimp and are just about at the bottom of the food chain. The swordfish would follow them up, I thought.

I saw a few inverted V's scattered between ten and fifteen fathoms, and my heart raced. Tuna. New regulations allowed me to have as many as I could catch. Old regs limited long-liners to one fish per trip, resulting in a few dead tuna being thrown back over the side (not much in the way of conservation). As tuna is more of a daytime feeder, we never catch that many of them while targeting sword. Giant bluefin tuna is sometimes worth its weight in gold. Fish that run between eight hundred and a thousand pounds each fill the fish hold quickly. I recalled a seven-hundred-pounder that I received thirty-five dollars per pound for, and I felt a happy flutter in my stomach. And bigeye tuna, although much smaller, were often very pricey. This was the time of year for the Grand Banks to produce tuna with high fat content, which usually rendered them more valuable than swordfish. Swordfish was our bread and butter. Any incidental tuna would be a bonus. If we landed a boatload of sword and a few tuna, we'd be fat.

Arch stuck his head in the back door and said, "We didn't get enough bait out of the freezer for eight hundred hooks. Should I thaw more out or cut it off at seven hundred?"

"This is looking really good, Arch," I said, indicating the sound machine. "Let's set nine hundred. I wasn't seeing much until I started down the east side of the canyon."

"Wow! Look at all of that bait!" Arch stared wide-eyed at the multicolored blobs that now filled the screen from fifteen fathoms to the surface. "Okay, I'll get a few more boxes thawed!" He hustled down the ladder and back to the deck, where I could hear his report to his shipmates over the intercom. "We're on 'em! She wants nine hundred. Mike, you keep throwing hooks, and, Tim, stay on floats while Dave and I get more bait up." Now everyone was feeling the excitement and anticipation for the haulback. If you've done it right, hauling longline gear can be like Christmas morning every time you pick up the end buoy. And now the guys sounded like a bunch of kids expecting rewards from Santa for good behavior. I could feel the men's kindled excitement through the steel deck. I was in my groove.

Although live bait is where it's at in most hook fishing, frozen bait is the only option for the distant-water fleet. I had made the huge mistake of thinking I could catch squid for fresh bait one winter while running the *Hannah Boden* out of Puerto Rico. The boss rigged the boat with automatic jigging machines and gigantic spotlights to attract the squid, which are caught at night. The problem was that the jiggers were less than automatic, and what they produced needed to be iced. So our four hours of sleep each night was cut to no sleep at all. We couldn't endure that schedule for long and were thrilled to go back to dead, frozen bait.

I was relieved that Arch had taken the reins on deck. I was also happy that he had come up and asked what to do about the bait shortage. It sometimes took a few nights to get a correct amount of bait thawed, as the boxes all contained a different number of individual fish. After a couple of sets, an average becomes obvious. I recalled a time many sets ago, late in a long trip, when we were all at the end of our wicks and the guys hadn't thawed enough bait. Rather than asking me, knowing I would say to get more out because we always set a thousand hooks, they decided to cut the gear off at eight hundred. They had the deck all cleaned up and were headed to their bunks while I continued to work, oblivious to their decision. I was still zigging and zagging along the break and thinking I was making one hell of a good set when I noticed that there was no gear going out. I insisted, much to the crew's dismay, that they get out more bait while I found the end buoy with a searchlight. We tied back in and set the remaining gear with long faces and complaints on deck. The following day the haul was one of the best ever. We totally plugged the fish hold and went home. I never said, "See? I told you so." But it was there.

Now, as it turned out, we ran out of line before we got all nine hundred hooks set. The drum was dangerously close to the bitter end when we cut the gear off. Although the many turns I made back and forth and around depth changes made it difficult to know exactly how many miles had gone over the stern, it seemed to me that we had set closer to thirty than forty. In fact, at an average speed of seven knots for four and a half hours, my math said approximately thirty-two miles. I had been told that the *Seahawk*'s drum held forty miles, and it appeared to be full. We didn't have any spare line stored aboard. Now it was clear that we would fish short sets for the trip. We had also set every single float on the boat. Oh, well. We would make do. We had real synergy going for us.

We would just have to be more productive with less gear, I resolved as I shut the boat down for the night. We could squeeze a thousand hooks onto thirty-two miles. I had to put the gear on the meat every night and not waste any line searching or exploring. We certainly couldn't afford to lose any gear. I had a reputation for *not* losing gear. I was good with the RDF and better with radar. One of my strong points was estimating where a loose piece of gear would be when parted off. I would pay extra attention to wind and tide this trip. We would have to be diligent about clearing all snarls. We would be fine with the bare minimums. My mojo was alive and doing fine.

I climbed into the top bunk knowing that I would not sleep. I had actually begun to believe what Sebastian Junger had written about me. I wasn't just the only woman in the business, I was one of the best captains, period, on the entire East Coast. Of course, I knew that the number of captains remaining in this racket was damned small. But still, no matter how poor the results, I must be *one* of the best. A combination of excited anticipation for the haulback and questioning whether the self-deceptive mode was working overtime had me wondering. Mostly what I wondered was why successful fishing at this point in my life was so important to me. Hadn't the standard by which I measured my own worthiness grown beyond seaworthiness? Apparently not, I admitted as I imagined hauling aboard the first fish in ten years. I was certainly aware of times when everything looks perfect during a set but nobody's home the next day. And I hoped the haulback would put to rest the possibility that I had seen tonight through rose-colored glasses. My reality check was just a few short hours away. Tomorrow would answer a lot of questions.

CHAPTER 9

The Grand Banks Bubble

Light westerly wind teased up the ocean's surface to just beyond ripples. The rising sun shone across and through, rather than down upon, the surface that flickered in flamelike, yellow squirming shimmers. It was unusually clear and calm for this late in the Grand Banks season. I had always been thankful for good weather. But more so today, since great conditions would be appreciated as the five of us ironed out wrinkles that had set in during a decade of storage. Mornings are gung ho at this longitude, fully alert and broadly lit while daylight to the west is still sleeping soundly. I had been up for an hour when I pulled on my knee-high rubber boots. As I stepped from the fo'c'sle onto the deck, I took in a gulp of cool air and exhaled a sigh of warm anticipation. This was day one in the persistence and determination that defined Linda Greenlaw. No matter what this haul produced—good or bad—it was only one day of many to come. Nevertheless, the first haul of any trip can be a defining pacesetter. A slow start could amount to a marathon, while a great day could mean a sprint to a quick finish. I had competed in a few hundred-yard dashes in my career. But most races required a little more leg and wind.

The first haulback would be primarily a physical test. I wondered if muscles had memory that could stretch to bridge a ten-year gap. Or would my physical ability be more like an old piece of pot warp left to dry out in the sun, faded and kinked beyond useful-ness? Although I'd been tending lobster traps since my departure from blue-water fishing, my inshore life on the water was tamer in many ways. When I wake up at home to a screeching gale, I pull the covers over my head and wait for a better chance to haul my traps, with a comfort level enhanced by the thought that the traps are getting an extra night to fish. That is not an option off-shore. If gear is in the water, it must be hauled back aboard or be lost. It's that simple. I am physically weaker than I was at thirty-seven. But I was confident that I could indeed work smarter and not harder, a combination that might make me more efficient than the younger, tougher me. This work would certainly lead to some sore muscles. I actually looked forward to some aches and charley horses. Like the emotional/psychological element, the physical component needed to fish for sword is more endurance than sheer strength. And I have always been more of a distance runner than a sprinter in terms of work.

Last night I'd given the crew the option of a wake-up call that would allow them time for breakfast. And all but Machado had agreed that they would indeed like to get up when I did. Machado wanted the extra thirty minutes in his rack, evidence that he was my only true veteran. I knew that the breakfast club would dissolve as the trip wore on and hunger was quickly upstaged by sleep deprivation. But this morning we ate oatmeal. I couldn't wait to leave the galley, as excitement mounted for what our first haulback would produce. If you're not excited for the very first haul, there's no hope. I had a reputation of being first on deck and last off when I worked as a crew member, and that attitude and persistence followed through my years in the captain's chair.

I took my position at the hauling station and looked upwind for the beeper buoy that marked the southeast end of our string of gear. I had steamed to the buoy just prior to inhaling my oatmeal. And sure enough, there it was, bobbing slowly and wagging its whip antenna. I put the engine in forward and jogged toward the buoy while the men watched and waited from their single-file lineup behind me along the port rail. Machado had not yet emerged into the light of day. Although it would have been nice to have him conduct very basic instruction to the others, I didn't actually need him until there was a fish on deck to be cleaned. Some guys are just unleadable. Machado might be one of the few who truly can't be pushed. Trying to light a fire under his butt could be counterproductive. Forcing, threatening, cajoling . . . My read of Machado so far was that nothing would work. Good thing I hadn't counted on him to set an example of a work ethic. And, I knew, the rest of the guys were all seasoned fishermen and had a good understanding of the process and procedures without ever having experienced long-lining for sword per se. We would get along fine without Machado. I hoped he'd come to life when a fish hit the deck.

The device used to steer the *Seahawk* from the hauling station was a jog stick, a small lever that sent an electrical signal that controlled the rudder. The jog stick was mounted on a steel plate next to the gearshift and throttle, where I could easily operate all with my right hand. The valve that drove the hydraulic main-line spool was just below the engine controls. And I could reach that with either hand, depending on what else I had going on. The men had built an eight-inch platform from some scrap wood for me to stand on while I hauled, without which the main line (as it is retrieved) would be too high for my five-foot-three stretch. I needed to be tall enough so that the hauling block, which was welded to the overhead, hung just above my left shoulder. Comfortable and effective hauling technique calls for the line to run over my shoulder and through my left hand while it comes out of the water so that I can grab or remove the snaps that attach the leaders to it and also to feel fish coming. I knew I would be a bit awkward at first, especially with the line rigged on the port side. But I'd hauled what I estimate to be tens of thousands of miles of longline gear in my life. So I assumed that I would adjust somewhat easily to being left-handed. Attitude would carry me until my rusty skill loosened up.

The beeper was alongside. I knocked the boat out of gear. Hiltz tossed a small grapnel to catch the line upwind of the buoy and pulled the rope tied to the grapnel hand over hand until he had the monofilament main line aboard. Timmy grabbed the line that was secured to the beeper and hauled the buoy aboard through the "door," or the cutout in the side of the hull through which fish are pulled. Timmy turned off and stowed the beeper in its spot in the steel rack along the starboard rail, while Hiltz coiled and stowed the grapnel. Archie cut the knot from the end of the main line meant to keep the beeper from sliding off the bitter end and, with a barrel knot, tied the end leading into the water to the end coming from the spool. Timmy took a wrap of line around his hand on one side of the knot, and Arch did the same on the other. The two 280-pound men each gave a heave in opposite directions to cinch the knot up tight. We were hooked up.

I pushed the gearshift forward, turned the jog lever to straighten the rudder, and twisted the valve to start the drum spinning. As the drum turned, it wound the line onto it. The line was pulled from the water, through the single-sheave hauling block behind and above my left shoulder, through a second identical block mounted at eye level on the setting house's forward bulkhead, and across the work deck onto the spool. My left hand rode the line as it came aboard, feeling for the right tension. I would go through a lot of left gloves, I realized. Too bad I hadn't saved all the lefts from the years of right-rigged hauling. At the end of a trip, the captain always has quite a collection of gloves for the nonhauling hand, while the other half of each pair has been totally destroyed and discarded.

I adjusted the throttle and the main spool's hydraulic valve to achieve the correct angle of line from hauling block to water, then tweaked the jog stick back and forth to get the correct angle in the other dimension of boat to gear. Hauling gear is not pulling all forty miles to the vessel, but rather driving the boat along the string while winding the line up and out of the water. A snap broke the surface. The leader was slack, indicating nothing on the hook. I grabbed the snap from the main line and handed it to Arch, who stood beside me at the rail. Arch clipped the leader to the messenger line that ran to the stern, where the leader was received by Dave Hiltz, who coiled it neatly into a box. "One down, seven hundred and ninety-nine to go," Arch said.

Hauling back is the time to ditch the rose-colored glasses you've donned while setting out and replace them with the 3-Ds. The physical realm of boat and gear is all-dimensional. The line wanders around just below the surface in every direction on the compass and at different depths. And the boat follows it left and right, but in rough weather it may go up on a wave and down into a trough when the gear is doing the reverse. The emotional side of hauling gear is all up and down, and dramatically different. While the mental state during setting out is relatively buoyant, the mind makes so many transits through the multitude of psychological altitudes during the haulback that to refer to a roller coaster doesn't even come close. Constant retallying of our status, measured in a number of ways, is how we mark time during and along the hauling of the string.

I don't wear a wristwatch, never have. The time of day is insignificant (except for 10:00 A.M., when we're fishing among the fleet and radio checks become necessary). I don't often ask watch wearers for the time. I ask, "How many floats to the next beeper?" "How many fish did we have that section?" "How much did that fish weigh?" The answers to these and other similar questions are factored into the fluid equation of how things are going. If we catch three fish in the first section, I multiply that by ten and figure we'll have thirty for the day. If we catch nothing on the first section and four fish on the second, I figure either we'll average two fish per section or we'll have eight on the third and sixteen on the fourth. Of course, if the third section has nothing to show, I have to recalculate down to more realistic numbers. There is absolutely no fancy math in my method of marking or predicting. Yet it's as accurate as any other formula would be. Although there is no way of knowing until the last hook comes aboard how successful the set was, that has never stopped me from averaging, multiplying, and speculating. The 3-D glasses are worn from the first hook to the very last, up to the tippity-top of every hope and down to the pit of every disappointment. The only certainty is that there is no certainty. I learned that the hard way, and it's the only thing I really know about fishing.

For the next six or seven weeks, we would be living in the Grand Banks bubble, which has its own bizarre relation to time. Most of my nineteen-year offshore career had been spent in that bubble, and I now realized that the ignorance and protection afforded by the total envelopment in a world apart was a lifestyle that I had chosen, too, by residing on the tiny, remote Isle au Haut. The island bubble is every bit as impenetrable from the outside as is the fishing bubble. Little news filters through from the world outside. The only news that's considered worthy is that generated from within. When I was at sea, I wouldn't be touching base with the island and they wouldn't waste their time wondering what was happening here. Time of day and day of week were of no consequence out here in the middle of the North Atlantic Ocean. What mattered were how many gallons of fuel remained in our tanks and how old the bottom of the trip, or first fish caught, was. Days were not scheduled around mealtimes. Meals were taken when there was opportunity, regardless of the hour, the number of hours since the last meal, or gnawing hunger. Lunch was not included in the Grand Banks vocabulary. A candy bar or a bag of chips could be gobbled during haulback while you were searching for the end of gear that had been severed by a ship, chewed by a shark, or stretched beyond breaking strength by the tide, making part-offs disconcertingly welcome late in the afternoon.

Life in the Grand Banks bubble did not require a calendar. Here there exist none of the constant shoreside reminders of holiday gifts to buy, appointments to schedule, or medications to ask your doctor about. There was no sudden shock of realization that you had forgotten to pick the dog up from the vet, water the plants, or get the car serviced. There was no church service, no minute of silence, no day of rest. Although men of the sea are prayerful at times, worshipping of gods is antisocial, personal, and soundless, done in absence of the nudge from Sunday. During this trip a presidential election would take place, and we wouldn't vote, and the results hardly caused a ripple—literally—in our waters. People could die, be buried and eulogized, without our ever hearing that they'd been sick. During the course of some careers on the Grand Banks, babies of friends and family had been conceived, been born, and graduated from high school, and nary a gift was ever sent. This was the epitome of existing in the moment, I thought, the here and now. We would live, breathe, eat, and sleep swordfishing. Being nonparticipants in the larger world is twofold. Fishermen are absent from that world much of the time, and even when present, they don't seem to care.

Within fifteen floats I was completely comfortable in the physical dimensions of driving and hauling as a southpaw. The orange floats suspending the line at five fathoms below the surface and marking the gear came alongside faster and faster. I pulled snaps and steered float to float like someone playing a game of connect the dots. Although we weren't catching anything, I would describe my mood as one of total bliss. I like hauling gear, because I do it well. Setting the gear out is the most important part of my job. It's where the financial payoff is. But hauling the gear is what keeps me coming back. Of course, hauling gear is more exciting when fish are being caught. But I enjoy the process. Like shooting a single birdie in many eighteen-hole rounds of golf, the feeling I get during haulback erases whatever badness has preceded. Hauling longline gear is fun—plain and simple. I would prefer to haul forty miles of blank sword gear than to pull traps full to the doors with lobsters. That's not to say I don't care about money. I do. I love money. In fact, I need money just like everyone else. And when I'm making money fishing for sword on the Grand Banks of Newfoundland, there's nothing better. Don't we all dream of making money doing what we love? How many of us actually get to try? Although it's fatiguing, especially in heavy weather, I have never regarded hauling longline gear as work. Hauling gear is really *driving* the boat, rather than riding aboard it with the autopilot engaged. Now, as I was turning the rudder to starboard to follow the gear around a corner, the deck moved under my feet at my command. Leaning into the port rail with my left hip, my legs pushed the *Seahawk* away and around the bend back to port. I've never been on a surfboard, but I suspect that it's the same sensation in a miniature version.

Machado graced us with his sleepy-eyed presence shortly after we began the second section. "Bring 'em on, Linny," he said, smiling. "I'm ready!" He spit on a sharpening stone and ran a knife in and out of the goo until it was honed to his specifications. Things were going smoothly. The crew hustled to coil leaders and wind ball drops onto their small spool. Except for there being no fish yet, this was as happy as I could be. I now knew that we could run to the east and fall into a position among the fleet. All we had to do was wind up the rest of the gear. We would be done when the sun reached its peak, and headed to where the big fish live. I had never before been skunked, and I knew that today would not be a first in that department. We still had many miles to haul, and the set had looked too good to come back empty.

"Fish on!" I yelled as the line tightened and the angle out of the water increased. I stopped the drum from turning, threw the boat out of gear and then into reverse, stopping our forward motion so that the taut leader was completely vertical and directly beside me. The heavy snap created a sharp V in the main line that moved along the line as the snap slipped with the fish tugging down and away. "It's green. Get gaffs," I said, referring to the fact that the fish was indeed lively and would need to be gaffed when I managed to finesse it up close enough to the surface.

"What is it?" Hiltz asked as he stood poised with a ten-foot gaff pole, ready to strike.

"Swordfish," I said confidently. And I knew it was, even though I hadn't seen what was now tugging the line deeper. I just knew from experience how a swordfish acts on longline gear. The fish was taking the line deep. A shark would run line on the surface, and a tuna either would be pulling much harder or circling or would have sunk a bunch of gear. The difference is difficult to articulate. But once you've felt a few fish, there's no mistaking a sword for anything else. Sharks and tuna just feel and act completely different. I opened the valve to turn the spool slowly and soon had the snap out of the water again and within my reach. Arch reached for the snap. "Leave it on the line. If the fish takes off, we won't lose it or pull the hook." I wanted badly to haul the fish myself. But with Archie being the age he was, and with the experience he had "wiring" fish, I just couldn't brush him aside the way I always had younger crew in the past. Arch squeezed the leader with one hand, then the other. He pulled with his back, gaining a few feet of the monofilament aboard with each bend and twist at his waist. The slack mono fell at his feet. He stopped pulling when the fish decided to dive, and allowed the slack to run through his hands and back into the water. When the fish stopped, Arch began again. I took the opportunity to instruct Hiltz in what Arch was doing right, knowing that Hiltz would be wiring live fish at some point. "All you can pull with one hand. And never take a wrap. Let the slack fall onto the deck. But don't ever move your feet."

Like two players in a game of tug-of-war, Arch and the fish went back and forth with the leader for some time. When the leader began swimming in circles rather than diving straight down, I knew that Arch had the upper hand. In the fifth death circle, I saw a flash of color that sent my heart into overdrive. "Nice fish! Next circle, when it comes out from under the boat, it should be close enough to gaff. Make sure you get it in the head," I instructed both Tim and Dave, who now waited anxiously on either side of Archie. The fish came out from beneath the hull. Two gaffs were sunk expertly into its head simultaneously. The men led the fish aft a few feet to the door and pulled it onto the deck. Silver, pink, and blue, the fish's sides glistened in the sun. Its back was royal blue, darkening to nearly black in the dorsal fin. The fish flopped a couple of times the way fish do, and then lay motionless. The grape-Popsicle purple pigment ran out of its bill with the last pump of its gill plate. I restrained my emotional high, knowing that we had many miles of possible lows to navigate. But in my mind's eye, I pumped a fist.

Machado severed the sword from the head with a meat saw, then the head from the body. Blood spurted and then ran in a small stream onto the deck, forming a thick puddle that was washed away with the deck hose and out a scupper. I estimated the weight to be around 150 pounds, said, "Good job," and turned my attention back to the controls and hauling. I couldn't wait to feel the next sword. The men stood and admired the beautiful fish. We had come a long way to get to this point. There were some high fives behind me and some very relieved voices. Arch pulled a camera out of nowhere and snapped a few pictures as Machado gutted and cleaned the magnificent fish. I wished the men would hurry back to their respective stations, but I remained quiet while they reveled in the glory of their first fish. So maybe we could do this.

"Greenhorn! Time for the greenhorn's initiation!" Machado announced as he pushed the swordfish's heart toward Hiltz. "You have to eat the heart. Otherwise we'll have bad luck." We all laughed at the prospect of bad luck in light of how unfortunate we'd been so far. Hiltz grabbed the heart and took a bite out of it as he would an apple. He chewed and swallowed, smiled and went for another bite. Before he could sink his teeth back into the heart that was still pulsating in his hand, Arch batted it away, issuing a warning about getting sick. Hiltz chuckled as he wiped blood from his black-bearded chin with the back of his glove. I was sure that he would have consumed the entire heart. He actually looked like he'd enjoyed the bite he managed to get down before Arch intervened. I turned back to the hauling station, glad I didn't have to witness any more of the eating ritual. I recalled many a greenhorn puking at the rail at just the thought of nibbling a heart freshly cut from a fish.

"Hey, Linny!" Arch yelled. I turned to see him aiming his camera at me. I flashed a big, cheesy, toothy smile, then quickly turned my attention back to the job of getting the gear aboard. I hauled and clipped leaders to the messenger line as the men continued to ogle the fish. Hiltz made a comment about his only desire being to catch fish, and we all laughed. I had never known such a feeling of relief. Sure, I was excited to see the fish. But the feeling of freedom from worry was much stronger. We were able to haul the gear. Machado was already placing a tail strap on the fish with which to lower it into the hold and pack it in saltwater ice. The evil spell was broken. The demons that haunted the *Seahawk* had been exorcised with the letting of sword blood on deck. We had caught a fish. I love my job, I thought.

"Shark!" There was no mistaking a leader that held a menacing blue shark. They nearly always swim to the surface. I caught a glimpse of the tail fin as it poked above the top of the water. It was limp rather than rigid like that of a sword. I grabbed the snap from the main line without stopping the boat or the drum and pulled the leader until the shark was right against the hull. Bluish gray with a white underside. I hoped we wouldn't see many of these. There's no market for blue sharks, and when they come in numbers it can be a huge nuisance, as they chew up the gear. "Cut it off as close to the hook as you can," I said while Arch leaned over the rail with a knife. The weight of the shark being towed made the monofilament stretch tight and kept the shark's head above the surface. One touch with the knife to the leader and the shark swam off with a circle hook in its lower jaw. The hooks we use are made of fairly soft, inexpensive steel that rusts away quickly. Even so, I had caught sharks in the past that sported as many as three hooks sacrificed by other fishermen. So I've decided that blue dogs (as we call them) are either very hungry or very dumb.

No sooner had the shark disappeared than there was another one pulling a leader to the surface, this time swimming under the boat rather than away. I hauled. Archie cut. Then there was another. Next came a shark that would rival Jaws; he was a size that fishermen would call a 747. I took the engine out of gear to give Archie time to deal with shark number three before jumping in to handle jumbo number four. The next half section had a fiendish brute on every hook. When the sharks come "hookety-hook," the hauling is slowed to a crawl. I had the boat out of gear as we cleared leaders twisted up with ball drops and cut sharks out of tangles they had rolled themselves into. I silently prayed for relief from the blue devils, hoping that each swing around a corner might lead to a different depth or temperature that these particular monsters might find unappealing.

The beeper marking the end of the third section had two sharks wound up tight with it. I backed the boat down to make it easier to haul the mess aboard. We cut a huge snarl out of the main line and tied back in. Any longline fisherman who has encountered blue dogs of this size in this number has an understanding of "shark attack" that does not include missing limbs. It's frustrating, in a vicious-circle kind of way. The slower you go, the more time sharks have to find an empty hook. And the more sharks that find a hook, the slower the going. When I proceeded to the next shark, the boat didn't go in the direction I wanted. The rudder indicator showed hard over to starboard, but the jog stick was to port. "I've lost steering," I said to Arch as I pulled the engine out of gear.

"Timmmaay!" Arch yelled, a little louder than necessary. "There's no steering!" Timmy hustled up the deck and disappeared toward the engine room. We drifted for a few minutes, waiting for a report from below. As we waited, I remembered a trip early in my career when the broken deck steering could not be repaired. It was back aboard the *Walter Leeman*. I was nineteen years old and learning my way around the deck on my very first haulback when the captain, Alden Leeman, announced that someone would have to steer the boat from the wheelhouse until we were able to retrieve the rest of the gear. I was assigned the job of steering while being screamed at from below. Keeping the boat exactly where the captain wants it to be in relation to the gear in fifty knots of wind on your first trip is a chore. The steering was in no way "power," and it required a bit of strength to spin the wheel back and forth. I don't recall how long it took me to realize that I could aim the boat toward the next float off the bow rather than zigging and zagging hard over to hard over among shouted orders laced with obscenities from below, but I guess by the end of that very long day I had figured it out. Alden, popularly known as "Screamin' Leeman," refused to go ashore for repairs. So I spent every haulback in the wheelhouse. I suppose that I had learned at least part of my stubborn persistence on that trip. I now hoped that history wouldn't repeat itself, as I did not look forward to the prospect of sending Arch up to steer from the bridge while I hauled from below.

Timmy appeared back on deck. "The breaker was tripped. We

should be okay now," he said as he joined me in watching the rudder indicator while I moved the jog stick. Things seemed to be in
order again. I shrugged. Timmy shrugged and hurried back to his
post in the stern, where he was trying to repair sharked-up leaders fast enough to keep pace with the cutting spree that continued at and aft of the hauling station. Leaders from which sharks
had simply been cut off needed a new hook crimped onto their
ends. Leaders that had done battle and suffered chafed and
stretched monofilament were cut to a shorter length to eliminate
their weakness. When a leader was determined unrepairable, the
hardware was spared and the line was discarded. Hiltz was working as fast as he could, as was Timmy.

Sharks just kept coming, sometimes two and three at once, all
in a balled-up mess of leaders, ball drops, and main line. The blue
bastards had struck with a vengeance. We lost steering again.
Timmy ran below, reset the breaker, and returned. Arch, Machado,
and I pulled manageable sharks over the rail, large ones through
the door, and cut the biggest of them off at the waterline. We removed and saved hooks when possible. I wished I had more hands
as I steered, hauled, pulled, and cut. The novelty of catching
sharks had worn thin for the crew. The fascination and intrigue
with the mystery and danger disappeared when the deck was
cluttered and expensive gear was being destroyed. My inexperi-
enced crew now handled the blue dogs as well as the most weath-
ered I'd ever worked with. Hiltzie kicked a shark out the door with
the toe of his rubber boot as he hauled another over the stern.
Archie walked through the gauntlet of twisting coils of flesh and
fins while snapping jaws tried to sink teeth into anything within
reach as casually as he would have passed through a flower gar-

den. The war games and crimes against sharks had not yet begun. But I knew they would.

Crews from the past had made contests of pounding sharks with ice mallets, like trying to ring the bell at the county fair, in attempts to stun the dogs long enough to remove hooks. At times of poor fishing and heavy sharking, mallets were swung and brought down out of frustration, or even for entertainment value. I remembered well the torture rack, the drawing and quartering, and the igniting with lighter fluid and running up the flagpole. I remembered embarrassingly fondly the games of shark-nose baseball. Maiming, torturing, and killing sharks out of frustration and some weird sense of retaliation or revenge were bound to occur. Perhaps not today, but sometime. Call it maturity, or a different philosophy, or appreciation for life in general—my attitude about living things had changed. Killing fish was okay, though. Doing so was to benefit an increasingly obese and heartsick population by supplying a healthy and sustainable food source. When the torture of blue sharks began—and I knew it would—I would nip it in the bud. I wouldn't have to pin the ban against senseless killing on a newfound love of all of God's creatures—nobody would buy that. I could simply use personal safety as the means to stop it. I had witnessed many a man suffer a nasty yet nonlethal shark bite, often in the course of shark warfare. Sometimes the shark wins.

We lost steering again. This time Timmy was longer in the engine room. "I'm trying another circuit breaker. Maybe the other one is going bad," he said. "We should be okay now." Timmy's dark bangs slashed across his forehead at a steep angle, giving him an air of consternation that I found misleading. What I knew of Tim Palmer was that he was solid, smart, and reliable. I added "strong" to his list of attributes as he effortlessly jerked the biggest shark of the day from the water and onto the deck while he explained his opinion of the steering problem. "The three-phase motor might be failing. That would cause the breaker to trip. I don't think we have a spare motor. I'll search when we finish hauling."

I hoped that the steering malfunction was something less severe than a bad hydraulic motor or pump. A replacement was a very expensive and unlikely item to have on board, seeing as the *Seahawk*'s supplies didn't even meet our more basic needs. I eventually noticed that I lost steering whenever the rudder was hard over to either side and the engine was in reverse. Perhaps I could try using less rudder. Maybe I was oversteering. I would certainly need full rudder in poor weather conditions. But if I anticipated more, I could probably stay on the gear with less rudder angle well enough to get the rest of the gear aboard. I kept this in mind, and the rudder functioned properly through the next barrage of blue sharks. When the entire deck was filled with writhing pests waiting to be freed from their monofilament lashings and pushed back overboard, Hiltz asked, "Is this normal?"

"No. We don't normally lose steering every time I back the boat down," I answered somewhat sarcastically. "It's gone again. Timmmaay!" And this time the rudder-angle indicator pointed at a very shallow fifteen degrees starboard. I was now measuring progress by the number of sharks we boarded, dehooked, and released between steering failures. My arms were weary, and my hands were sore from hauling on the heavy leaders. This was getting old. I had come crashing down from the initial emotional high to good old reliable determination. We would struggle. But we would get the gear aboard and head for greener pastures.

When the guys were all too busy behind me to cut off a shark from a leader I had pulled, I wrapped the leader around my waist to free my hands, towing the shark from my midsection while I continued to haul. At one point I had three sharks in tow, the leaders cinched around my waist like a corset. This gave my wrists some relief, as I realized they did indeed ache. Arthritis? A little pain was the least of my problems. We would have to figure out the steering situation. But for now I just wanted to get the gear out of the shark-infested water and head east to fish among the fleet. The guys could repair and replace all the sharked-up leaders while we steamed tomorrow. Timmy and Archie could work on the steering problem and have that solved before we set out again. I had it all figured out. We landed very few swordfish along the miserable way. I had tallied half a dozen so far. Fairly slow fishing. The fish were all markers, or over a hundred pounds each. A nice run—just not enough of them to fight the blue dogs for. Yet in spite of the sharks and steering, I was happy doing my thing. I would be happier when my thing included more fish and fewer sharks. But that would come in time.

We were just beyond two-thirds of the way through the gear. The sharks were as thick as ever. The angle of the sun indicated that we were well into the afternoon. The men were laughing. I turned to hear the joke. Timmy leaned with both hands on the rail and stared into the water. He broke into his best Jacques Cousteau imitation: "The lonesome blue shark is a solitary preda- tor. They do not swim in schools. . . ." Our deck was littered with sharks. Arch tossed one over the rail while I slung the next one aboard, perpetuating the continuous loop of teeth and fins. On and on Timmy went about blue sharks and how they always travel as singletons. Timmy had sharks surrounding his feet. He bent and started flinging them overboard by their tails, all the while going on about the "antisocial creatures that are never seen in numbers." Soon the rest of the crew were feigning French accents and lecturing on blue sharks' monastic habits.

Fortunately, when things are incredibly bad at sea, humor reigns. I was thankful and relieved to hear the men joking around. I'm not a pouter or a whiner, and I can't appreciate grown men who are either. The men would never hear me lamenting tired legs, sore hands, strained back muscles, or aching wrists, although I was feeling all of the above. Fortunately, it appeared I had a crew full of class clowns. They kept working and laughing. These men seemed not to possess the hostile gene that would have driven others to some form of shark hockey by now. There's nothing worse than sour attitudes and long faces. If the guys could enjoy a sharking of this magnitude, they'd surely be able to endure anything this trip could dish out. I had experienced much worse, countless times. The worst of all was when my relentless positivity failed to infiltrate a rotten crew. This hadn't happened often, as more than likely the crew will follow the captain's lead in physical and emotional ways. Good men will always keep up with their captain. And my present company were really proving themselves as we waded through the never-ending parade of sharks. At least the weather was cooperating. And we were making steady progress. Machado had actually broken out in song. By now I'd forgiven his late start. Bucking up in rough going was far more important than being an early bird.

We were picking our way through the sharks and looking forward to seeing the end buoy when a yellow and green airplane buzzed us. I recognized the familiar colors and markings as the Canadian fisheries patrol. I waved and continued to haul. The plane passed over us again. When it came by the third time, I thought I had better go up to the bridge and listen to the VHF radio. Someone might be in trouble and in need of assistance. Planes are good because they can cover a lot of area quickly, but they can't do much to help a boat in distress. I knocked the *Seahawk* out of gear, removed my gloves, giving them a twist to wring the water out of them, and hustled to the bridge. If I'd been aboard the *Hannah Boden,* I would have shed my oil pants before entering the wheelhouse. I hesitated for a second at the threshold of the back door. The plane was over us again.

Leaning in, I could see the electronics. I was immediately horrified by what I saw. The plotter showed the blinking boat symbol that represents the *Seahawk* on the wrong side of the Canadian fisheries line. I took two steps and stood directly in front of the computer monitor, staring in disbelief. I moved the cursor to the blinking boat as my stomach tied itself into a knot. We were nearly five miles into Canadian waters. I tried to force my blood pressure down by telling myself to remain calm—it couldn't be as bad as I thought—but I could actually feel the pounding in my neck. In all of my years of fishing experience, this was new and forbidden territory. I bit my lower lip and closed my eyes briefly. When I opened my eyes, nothing had changed. I was in deep trouble.

CHAPTER 10

Busted

For several numb-limbed seconds, I stood awestruck at the mysterious conspiracy of wind and tide that had pulled off such a covert and hateful caper. How could this have happened? The mixing of the Gulf Stream and Labrador Current in this region, which makes it so rich in fish, is also responsible for something called North Atlantic Drift, a prevailing current or tide that moves south and east on the west side of the bank—not north. The current was supposed to take the gear away from the Canadian fishing boundary and into the safety of international water, not into the most heavily patrolled and fervently regarded grounds on planet Earth. I manipulated the computer's mouse to move the crosshairs-style cursor across the electronic chart, stopping on the dotted line representing Canada's two-hundred-mile limit at the point closest to our present position due south of us.

The digital display confirmed that the *Seahawk* was better than four miles over the line of demarcation.

Big on personal responsibility and accountability, I tried to figure out what I'd done wrong. Where had I made a misstep? The knot in my stomach moved up to my chest, and my muscles tightened like those of a hunted animal in a fight-or-flight reaction. I looked again at the red line signifying last night's set and reluctantly removed my hand from the panic button. Okay, I thought, I have been seen and probably photographed fishing in Canadian waters. It wasn't intentional. I'll just have to deal with it. I certainly can't pretend not to be here. I am aboard a sixty-three-foot steel boat, and the weather is crystal clear. Yet another first in my return to the Grand Banks fishery—this was something I'd never even imagined could happen to me. But had it *happened* to me? Or had I somehow unknowingly brought this on myself? The captain is ultimately responsible for everything. Perhaps I'd been negligent in not running up to the wheelhouse to check our position. But drifting north had not been in the realm of possibility. I must be guilty of something, I thought shamefully.

Friends of mine had been in similar situations in the past. And I had never been very sympathetic, thinking that they'd been foolish to take such a chance as to fish too close to the "fence." My careless and guilty friends had received the proverbial slaps on the wrist for the same violation and had been told to get their hooks out of Canada and never return, or else. I would have to buck up and explain the situation and take my slap. I silently rehearsed my initial call. I was feeling like something between a total idiot and the victim of a cruel joke played by Mother Nature.

I can't remember ever deliberately breaking a law or rule. Even as a kid, with the knowledge that my maternal grandmother had advised my mother that I was one of those children who just could not be spanked, I never took advantage of that freedom by misbehaving. With the exception of the time I nearly burned the neighborhood out with a campfire gone bad, I had never been reprimanded. And even then I was actually trying to cook a hot dog and had not meant that to require three alarms. I defended myself and threw my pal Scotty Sturtevant under the bus. He had lit the match. My sister Rhonda had regarded me as a goody-goody and was pleased that I had temporarily joined her in her usual state of being in trouble with our folks. I never got grounded the way Rhonda did. I never wore the dunce cap at school or visited the principal's office. In adulthood I had formed a personal opinion that there are far too many laws, rules, and regulations. But I didn't protest or object to their enforcement. I wondered how my relationship with rules and the law might change with this new development. With a shove from the most threatening roar of the plane's engine yet, I reached for the VHF radio's microphone. Hesitancy was overcome by the knowledge that I hadn't intended to be here. Canadian law must certainly include a clause regarding intention. I hadn't actually done anything illegal, I told myself. Now was the time to buy stock in the notion that honesty was indeed the best policy. All I had to do was tell the truth.

"The fishing vessel *Seahawk* calling the Canadian fisheries plane. Channel sixteen. Come in, please. Over." It was something of a relief to hear my own voice sounding professional and not frightened (although I surely was) or guilty. A man replied with some official numbers of the plane and a radio call sign, then asked if I was hauling gear. He sounded sort of mad, as in angry. I responded that I was lying to, drifting with the engine disengaged. He repeated his question about whether I was fishing, and his tone was now accusatory, as if I had lied about hauling gear. I wondered whether I *had* just lied. Technically, I was not hauling at this time. I got nervous and began my explanation, which I'm sure sounded like the improvised alibi that it was.

"Are you hauling gear? Do you have gear in the water? Are you engaged in hauling gear at this time? Have you been hauling gear?" He was certainly persistent with this line of questioning.

"No, I am not hauling at this time. The engine is out of gear, and we are drifting. Over."

"*Seahawk*, are you fishing now? Do you have gear in the water? Were you retrieving your line when the plane was over you?"

I took a deep breath and held it in until my lungs simmered. I clutched the radio's mike at my side, unable to put it to my mouth. As I exhaled, my hand came up, and I keyed the mike. "Yes. Over." There, I had given him the answer he so desperately needed. "But I didn't realize that I'd drifted into Canadian waters. I made a legal set last night. I have been working below since four-thirty this morning, and I don't have any navigational equipment at the deck helm station. The boat has a steering problem, and we have been struggling with blue sharks. Over." Now I thought I sounded as if I were making lame excuses.

"Stay where you are. Do not continue to haul your gear. A Canadian coast guard ship is en route to you and will be on position in several hours. Over."

Several hours? This really sucked. All the anxious steam that had built up hissed out in short, choppy breaths, and I whispered to myself, "Jesus Christ, what next?" My neck had gone limp, allow-ing my head to hang. I closed my eyes and tried to concentrate on what I might be able to say to the man in the plane to gain his sympathy. How do speeders talk their way out of tickets? If only I could write a letter as I had to the FCC when I was facing a fine for inadvertently transmitting on a forbidden radio frequency. I'm so much better on paper than I am live, I thought. And although it is true that I was recorded chatting on the same banned frequency on the same day the FCC received my groveling correspondence, I was only doing so to explain to the man on the other end why we had to switch to something more legal. Of course, that required a second letter. But it worked. My thoughts were interrupted with another transmission from the plane's radio, asking if I had un-derstood that I was not to move or continue to retrieve gear. "Roger. Over." Volume and emphasis trickled out of my voice with these final two syllables. Archie had come up the ladder and stood at the back door. "Did you hear all of that?" I asked.

"Yeah. Don't worry, Linny. We'll be all right. My hands needed a break from wiring sharks anyway. I'll tell the guys what's going on." I hoped Arch was right. I knew that he was probably correct that we'd be fine. But in the meantime we had to wait several hours with about ten miles of gear remaining to be hauled. I real-ized that our situation was not dire. No one's life was at risk. We were not sinking or on fire. So our progress to the east would be delayed one more time. We would get there, eventually.

I joined the men on deck and added my opinion of what was yet to come to what Arch had already explained. The men all ral-lied behind me with indignation that we had to be detained by the authorities while I had been so diligent about doing drift tests and everything. Certainly I was not to be held responsible for what could only be explained as an act of God. The men had all seen the set I'd made on the plotter the night before. It was perfectly legal. I had done everything right. There was no explanation for our present illegal position other than the fact that we were aboard the *Seahawk*. The men all understood that I had nothing to hide, and neither did they. As soon as the ship came, I would simply continue to tell the truth and get myself off this inconvenient hook. "They're probably just trying to scare us by making us wait," Machado offered. "They want you to sweat a little."

I hoped that Machado's assessment was accurate. I worried about my reputation in the world of fishing. The only time I had almost been in trouble aboard a boat was when a disgruntled crew member had ratted me out for having a few illegal shark fins aboard. The evidence was found when fisheries patrol searched a small hidden compartment after they'd been tipped off. The contraband fins had been aboard and forgotten about when the regulations had changed, requiring fishermen who harvest fins to have the shark's carcass aboard, too. I successfully explained my way out of that one—it only cost me ten pounds of fresh fish. Of course, that was before I was portrayed in Warner Bros.' blockbuster *The Perfect Storm*. I wondered if that notoriety might be a factor in any decisions being made by the authorities. I hoped not.

I placed my left hand on the main line that was now getting way too tight with the strain of the boat drifting away from the remaining unhauled string. We had hauled about two-thirds of the gear at this juncture, leaving ten miles in the water. I backed off the drum a bit to lessen the strain and avoid parting off the line. This did nothing to relieve the ever-increasing stress I was feeling in my shoulders and neck. The plane buzzed again, and I realized that the airborne authorities above might mistake what I'd just done for hauling gear. I didn't dare put the boat in forward to jog up on the line in order to keep it slack. I decided that I would need permission to cut the line and mark it with a beeper to be retrieved after we straightened out this predicament. We could not drift like this, hooked up to the line, for several hours without creating more problems for ourselves. Drifting with gear trailing along under strain always resulted in spin-ups and part-offs. Things were difficult enough with steering woes and sharks—I didn't need to go multiplying them with greater hassles. I went to the wheelhouse to radio my intentions and ask permission to sever the gear from the boat at this time.

My request to cut and mark the gear was met with skepticism. Surely the men aboard the plane had dealt with bad characters in the past and were now paranoid that I must have something in mind other than what I'd stated. They must have taken many pictures by now of the *Seahawk* engaged in illegal fishing. Did they think I would cut and run? Of course, there's a chance that it was my own paranoia and not theirs that I sensed. The man on the radio put me on standby while he called his supervisor. The plane made steeper and steeper banks over us, seemingly afraid to let us out of its sight. I knew that the people up there had protocol to follow. These guys were just doing their jobs. Finally word came back that allowed me to cut the gear from the boat, along with another warning not to haul the gear or move the boat. I thanked the man and relayed to my crew an order to clip on our strongest beeper and cut the line. Now we had nothing to do but wait. And worry.

What would Alden do? Well, to begin with, he would have flipped the plane the bird on its first pass. Alden would never have left the deck to call the plane. He would have continued to haul until the end buoy was aboard. Then he would have faced the consequences behind the shield of a high-powered attorney. Alden had a lot of experience on the wrong side of the law. And he always wiggled his way out of trouble, never admitting that he might possibly have made a mistake. Too late for that. Besides, that wasn't my style. I had a real and heartfelt belief in the power of telling the truth. That, coupled with the fact that I've never been a good liar, eliminated any other option. Not that I considered Alden a liar, but he did have a way of shading things a degree or two. Full disclosure had never failed me in the past. Any reasonable person, Canadian or other, would see that I had not intended to be on the wrong side of any boundary line. Besides, we weren't exactly depleting the Canadian swordfish stock. My mental tally was at six. I guessed that I did deserve to be waylaid and inconvenienced, and I hoped that would be the extent of my punishment for what I'd managed to convince myself was no fault of my own.

The more I thought about it, the better I felt. I'd always had a great deal of respect for authority. I had dealt with the Canadian coast guard and fisheries department over the radio since I began fishing the Grand Banks nearly thirty years before. Every transit through Canadian waters coming and going had been announced and allowed with friendly civility. All interaction with Canadian fishermen had been the same. I would characterize my relationship with Canadians as great. I'd been in and out of Canadian ports my entire career. I'd been in the business long enough for the Canadian officials to recognize my name and my reputation for obeying and respecting their laws and limits. The Canadians were just following protocol. Not to do so would appear to be treating me with favoritism. They had to treat me as they would a man in the same situation, I realized. I would wait patiently for the ship to come and send me on my merry way, the way they always did with men in the same situation.

It was time to place the dreaded phone call to Jim Budi back in Fairhaven. The anxiety I'd felt when delivering the news of our engine problem had multiplied tenfold. It was just my luck that the *Seahawk*'s satellite phone stayed connected long enough for me to get the facts out and short enough to eclipse any reaction from the other end. Now all I had to do was to sit and wait and let my mind imagine every worst-case scenario.

The man in the plane announced that they were low on fuel and headed to Newfoundland, reiterating that we were to remain here until the ship arrived to "deal with the situation." I answered that I understood, then sat back in the captain's chair to watch the horizon for the coast guard ship. As I scanned the crease between water and sky, my mind wandered to happier places. I missed home and faced my first regret for embarking on what was turning into a blue-ribbon disaster. I could be home, going through the doldrums of peacefully hauling a few lobster traps along the rocky shore, waving to a passing sailboater, wondering what my mother was making for dinner, and dreaming about being back offshore. I began feeling guilty for bringing four nice, responsible men along on this miserable trip. I was willing to bet that none of them had ever broken a fisheries law. Hiltz had never even received a speeding ticket, and Timmy made Hiltz look like a hardened criminal in comparison. I would have to get this conglomeration of events straightened out for the sake of sparing my crew's innocence.

I wondered who would believe that I'd never been in any trouble. Isn't that what we all say when we find ourselves there? I'm a decent and law-abiding person. I have never participated in what anyone could consider even the slightest misdeed. Unless you count the time I swiped a ball bearing from David Brown's desk in third grade. The teacher had us form a search party for the missing steel ball, and we were not to go out for recess until it was discovered. I miraculously "found" it under a radiator in the back of the classroom. David Brown was really happy. I was sure the teacher knew that I had stolen it, and I had to live with that deceit burning a hole in my otherwise honest being for the remainder of that school year. I had stolen and lied. But beyond that, I told myself, I had a clean record and conscience—until now.

But the longer I sat, the more incidents came to my attention through the cobwebs of the past. For someone who professes never to have crossed the line in word or deed, I sure seemed to be coming up with a lot of evidence to the contrary. Maybe I wasn't as squeaky clean as I once believed. And every time I'd done something wrong in the past, I'd been nabbed. Apparently *that's* the trend that had kept me mostly on the straight and narrow. If I'd believed that I would get away with a misdeed, I might just have tried more often. I now had to admit that I was a goody-goody not out of any moral or philosophical scrupulousness but rather out of fear of being caught and punished. Perhaps my self-image had been askew all these years. More likely, though, was the fact that I had surrounded myself with some real bad actors the length of my fishing career, in contrast with whom any normal person would ascend to sainthood.

I'd never worked with anyone guilty of a capital crime—that I was aware of. But drug-related charges and convictions, theft, and other forms of violent activity had seemingly been prerequisites for deckhands in the past. As long as my men followed the rules and laws of the ship, the only prior experience I was interested in was fishing-related. Granted, the rules I established were few: No drugs or booze or weapons allowed. And the cardinal sin of throwing plastic overboard was grounds for immediate dismissal. No sleeping on watch was strictly enforced and punishable by loss of pay. Other, smaller infractions, like fighting, resulted in fines levied. The fear of losing a paycheck had always kept the men somewhat in line. In my present situation, with my present company, I was beginning to question the upstanding perception I had maintained of myself through the years. Compared with my present crew, as opposed to men with whom I'd fished in the past, I looked quite culpable. The longer I sat, the more swollen my bag of guilt became.

The *Cygnus* came on the horizon at about 6:00 P.M., a rigid-looking vessel with strict red and white lines. The size and speed of the ship as she approached said no-nonsense. The captain radioed his intentions of coming within one quarter of a mile and launching an inflatable boat that would deliver the boarding party. The boarding party would consist of three men—two Canadian fisheries officers and one coastguardsman. The captain then explained that the three men would come aboard the *Seahawk* to do an investigation. I radioed that I understood and agreed to wait with my engine out of gear and drifting until advised to proceed. The coast guard had boarded my boats many times in the past. And my only concern back then had been whether any of my men would be taken from me for outstanding warrants or lack of legal citizenship—leaving me shorthanded to finish the trip. This time I knew that my crew was safe.

We watched—my crew from the deck and me from the back door of the bridge—as the ship's crew launched their small, hard-bottomed inflatable boat. Five men scrambled into the bright orange boat and headed toward us. As they came alongside, Arch and Timmy stood flanking the door with hands extended to assist the boarding party as they had to step up and onto the *Seahawk* from a moving platform. The officials waved my men away, refusing their friendly attempt at assistance. All the Canadians were armed, with guns strapped across chests that were clearly protected by bulletproof vests. They were certainly taking their jobs seriously. The inflatable peeled away and headed back toward the ship, while the three officers made their way up to the wheelhouse. Although I do not recall family names, I remember the head of the party introducing himself as Steve and the others as Terry and Dimitri.

Along with the introductions came a lot of what I assumed were boilerplate statements issued by Steve and required by Canadian law. I can't repeat the exact words, but the tone sounded a lot like being read your Miranda rights. I gave Dimitri permission to manipulate any or all of the electronics on the bridge he deemed necessary to conduct his part of the investigation. While he did his job, I answered questions asked by Steve, basically explaining how I came to my present circumstance. I told them about the drift test and how the results led me to make the set that I did. I explained the set and showed them the history stored on the plotter, which clearly indicated that I'd never entered Canadian waters during the setting of the gear. When Dimitri needed a diagram of my set to include in his evidence, I gave him a flash drive to copy it with. The questions continued, mostly the same stuff rehashed. Steve periodically made calls to his superior officer, who I assume was shoreside using a satellite phone, and he also radioed the ship from time to time.

Next in the Canadians' routine was the interrogation of my crew. Individually, my guys were asked to sit at the galley table and answer questions. I had already advised them to cooperate fully and to tell the truth, as we had no reason to do anything but. I can only assume that we all had the same story. One at a time, the men came to the bridge to report that they'd been questioned and to assure me that we were going to be fine. When the officers returned to the bridge, the crew went below to wait at the galley table and speculate about how much longer it would be before we were released and allowed to finish hauling our gear. Steve made a call on the satellite phone. Steve made another call. When he hung up from the second call, he said, "You're not going to like this."

"What?" I asked.

"I am placing you under arrest and seizing the vessel. I have been instructed to escort you to St. John's, Newfoundland."

CHAPTER 11

Legal Affairs

The *Seahawk*'s small wheelhouse was a tangle of legs that sprawled from folding chairs as the three men snored, heads back and arms crossed over uniformed chests that heaved in total discord. The authorities, who had been quick to tell me they'd been on their way home after two weeks of offshore duty when diverted to the scene of my transgression, slept soundly with the comfort of the two-hundred-foot *Cygnus* as a chaperone. I was surprised to be allowed to drive the boat after having been placed under arrest. (Goes to show what I know.) The exalted feeling I had reveled in while hauling gear—the epitome of being real and in the moment, here and now—was gone as if it had never existed. I now sat in the captain's chair and experienced the most bizarre, most surrealistic out-of-body experience. Some part of me was drifting dreamlike in a flood tide of confusion and emotion, while the rest of me went through the mechanics of captaining my boat. I was

oddly juxtaposed between maintaining command while in custody of what I regarded as an unknown, yet greater, authority.

The officials had agreed to allow us to haul what remained of
our gear. And we did so at daylight, landing another half-dozen
fish, which we were allowed to take. When a bitter end came aboard
with a mile and a half to go, I knew that a search for the missing
piece would be hopeless, with no functioning beeper to toll us in. I
made a halfhearted attempt to track the stray gear down and finally
gave up, knowing that this was a needle in a watery haystack. Besides, I had bigger problems to deal with. We were 240 miles from
St. John's, Newfoundland. So I figured I had at least thirty hours to
chat with Steve, Terry, and Dimitri, once they woke from their
naps, about what would happen to me when we hit shore.

Archie sneaked up the stairs and tipped an imaginary cup to
his lips, asking if I wanted coffee. I shook my head and stuck out
my lower lip in an exaggerated pout, indicating my mood, which
had blossomed into full-blown sadness from the sprouts of disbelief of the night before. Arch nodded and pulled a camera from
his breast pocket. We glanced at the Canadians' arsenal, which
they had piled haphazardly on the chart table, and then looked at
each other. Arch shook his head, then scowled at me for even
having the thought. It would have been a really cool picture, but I
let it go and went back to being sad and staring at the horizon
while feeling the chill of the shadow cast by the *Cygnus*, which
remained close by on our starboard aft quarter.

The situation was so foreign to my experience that I didn't
know how to act. I covered my awkwardness by concentrating on
the familiar. I focused on the weather and navigation and planned
a new fishing attack. When in doubt, go to what you know. I asked

Archie about the amount of damage the sharks had done to our leaders. He looked at me like I'd lost my mind. Then, as if humoring the crazy lady, he agreed to check with Hiltz and Timmy. I listened intently to the SSB radio for positions and fish reports from the boats working to the east and formed a strategy for squeezing into the lineup. When Archie reported a loss of three hundred leaders, I ordered the crew to begin rebuilding. "But, Linny, you're under arrest," Arch said, as if trying to wake me from a dream. I insisted that I didn't care where we were going and that we really needed to work on the gear. "The boat has been seized. We're going to Newfoundland." Arch spoke softly and kindly, as if I didn't quite understand my situation and he was trying to explain without upsetting me.

"Arch, get the crew on the gear. If you don't, I will."

"I'm on it." And away he went, looking a lot like a spanked puppy. I just couldn't have the crew thinking we were done. I had my doubts, but they needn't know. The only part of my world that was real and tangible was my command of my boat and crew. I would hold on to those with clenched fists. If I let go, everything would meld into the blur of the unknown and scary.

One at a time, the arresting officers shook themselves awake and stretched the stiffness from backs and knees with groans of pain. They were polite and courteous, as if paying a social visit on board, nothing at all like I'd assumed they would be. In spite of my present status—under arrest and in custody—they paid me the respect due to any captain. There were many transmissions in all directions on radios and satellite phones between the *Seahawk*, the *Cygnus*, Jim Budi, and someone I guessed to be the real boss and the one calling the shots, for whom I came to develop a strong dislike. The nameless authority was ordering the under-lings to do what they actually seemed uncomfortable doing and was a great target for my silent but growing feelings of fear and anger. From my support system came assurance that the problem was being handled and that I would be released and free to return to the fishing grounds before we closed in on St. John's. This was countered by my Canadian custodians, who relayed a skepticism that undermined the power of each encouraging update from Jim Budi. The struggle shoreside went back and forth, and intensity grew palpable in the frequent snippets shared.

There was no privacy in any conversation. I heard all "they" said. And they heard all that I said. I'm sure we deduced quite accurately the tone and content of the talk of higher-ups on each side of the equation. It became increasingly clear that I had landed in the middle of an International Incident, and that although I was the unintentional instigator, I had become a pawn. Whatever had transpired in the crossing of the boundary was now insignifi-cant. Principles overshadowed reality. Now the arresting officers and I sat on the sidelines and became spectators. A strange bond-ing took place. Like characters in stories of prisoners and their captors, we were forming a real and sympathetic rapport.

The Canadian men took turns going back to the *Cygnus* for meals, for showers, and to sleep in real bunks. The orange inflat-able kissed the side of our hull with each changing of the guard every six hours. When Terry returned to duty refreshed and clean-shaven, he confided that the ship's cook was a fan of my books and asked if I would be willing to sign copies he carried aboard. Terry was a bit embarrassed to ask, and I was a little shy about being asked under the circumstances. But I proudly scrawled my name across the title pages of three books, which Terry tucked away in his travel bag. The next time Terry went on leave, he returned with hot muffins for the crew and me. And later, when Steve stepped back aboard after his break from the tedious *Seahawk* watch, he delivered a large platter of fried chicken.

The Canadians carted all their own stores aboard the *Seahawk* and kept them on my chart table. I normally flipped out when a crew member placed food or drink in my workspace. But this was different. Even when a carton of fruit juice fell over and spilled sticky syrup that wicked under the glass and soaked my navigational chart, I wiped it up with a wad of paper towels and told my new friends not to worry about it. The Canadian men were quick to share food with us, not that we didn't have enough of our own. But theirs was more interesting. ("Interesting" should not be confused with "tasty.") When my crew and I complimented the extraordinary hardtack biscuits, even a single one of which, I was convinced, could be gnawed for days in a life raft, an entire case came aboard. The biscuits were a challenge for teeth and jaws but were a good source of entertainment in a weird sort of way. "No, dear. Don't crunch it like that. You'll surely destroy your dentals. Moisten a small bit, then chew" was the advice. I had always found patience with food a difficulty, so I didn't consume the stuff as intended. But I enjoyed it nonetheless. I much preferred hearing the crunch and feeling the sharp edges cut gums to the passive swallowing of mush. Eating hardtack was real. I might not have been in control of my immediate destiny, but no one could tell me how to eat.

The *Seahawk*'s owner, Malcolm MacLean himself, weighed in with strong words that bolstered my resolve. "The bond money required for your release is in place with the Canadian authorities. I have hired an attorney to represent us. You should be released and free to go fishing within the hour." This was a huge relief, as we still had several hours remaining in steaming to St. John's. That time would be better spent traveling in a different direction, one that would put us in the vicinity of the U.S. sword fleet. I waited for my company to receive the call from shore to set me free. It didn't come. They were ordered to remain aboard and deliver me to the government dock, where I would be met by customs, immigration, and fisheries. I waited for someone to have a change of heart or for them to come to their senses. Every mile that passed under our hull diluted my hope of bypassing what was sure to be a scene at the dock.

I spent some time getting to know my Canadian escorts. I learned about their families and hobbies. These were nice men doing their country proud with professionalism. There was absolutely no antagonism, no good cop/bad cop ploys. These are men I would have as friends. There was no talk of guilt or of breaking laws. These men, it seemed to me, believed me and regarded me as innocent of everything other than perhaps being a victim of circumstance. One of the men would have liked to go to court with me, he said, but he had a doctor's appointment. Two of the men talked about their upcoming retirement plans. One of them sang. His soft voice filled the wheelhouse with cozy, lilting Newfy sea chanteys. When he sang a ballad about the hardships of life at sea and harsh treatment by superiors, I felt as transparent as the gal in "Killing Me Softly."

My men were nothing less than stellar. They acted as the perfect hosts to our Canadian guardians, frequently offering refreshments from the galley and asking what they could do to help or to make the uniformed men more comfortable. They all engaged in conversation about topics ranging from fishing and hunting and cooking to politics. The Canadian men joined my crew at the galley table, where they shared laughs and coffee, leaving me alone in the wheelhouse for several joyous minutes at a time. When my crew came topside, they did so to reassure me. Arch was as protective as my father is, and the others acted like brothers. That night, when we were close enough to the dock to see the number of official vehicles and various armed uniforms there to catch our lines on the inside of a guarded gate and under large floodlights, my men vowed not to leave my side—no matter what. If anything happened to me, it would happen to us all. As we secured to the dock, my men and I shared looks and nods that were dramatic and emotional. The pervasive mood was one that I could only characterize as "They'll never take us alive." We were in this together. This cohesion, in my experience, had been seen only in times of peril brought on by heavy weather and when survival depended on it. We were no longer five individual beings, we were a single unit.

As the last line was made fast to a cleat at midship, the crowd milling about in the yellow light became still. I knocked the engine out of gear and hit the kill switch. The sound of the diesel winding down and into silence was accompanied by my helpless feeling of spiraling down the drain. The contented validity of the physical act of landing the boat had turned to the uneasy release of grip on my command and my personal reality. The hard and straight edges of my world had become fuzzy and indistinct. Authorities and officers seemed to float on and off the boat. Clipboards thick with forms were shuffled, read, and signed. Among the many poker faces reflected in badges were three smiles—on the faces of Jim Budi and the O'Briens, whom I remembered as our Canadian agents from years past.

My crew had been cleared by customs and immigration. Their temporary visas allowed them to remain in Canada for ten days. That hit home. Ten days? I'd been dreaming that I would turn the boat around tomorrow after clearing up this confused and mistaken mess. My crew was given permission to leave the boat. I was ordered to remain aboard and was introduced to the man and woman who would stand guard over me until the next morning at eight, when they would deliver me to the police station to be processed. The crowd disassembled, leaving me in the wheelhouse looking out the window at my guards, who looked back at me. There was no moment of raising a hand and simply explaining what had happened. Maybe tomorrow.

I had nothing to do other than try to sleep. My crew had all tucked in, with plans to accompany me through whatever was to come. I lay awake, staring at the overhead, which was too close for my eyesight to make sense of, and wondered what would become of all this. The situation was impossible! I still couldn't imagine where I had gone wrong. Yet, as was the gospel to my mind, the captain is ultimately responsible for everything aboard the ship. I had taken my eyes off the road. I should have paid more attention to the wheelhouse and left the deck to my crew. Had I miscalculated when I did the drift test? The Canadians were sure making a big deal out of a little aberration of tide. Why hadn't they arrested Mother Nature? Total bewilderment was eased ever so slightly by the hope that tomorrow would offer an opportunity for me to talk sense to someone.

A smudged sun crept hesitantly from a woolly darkness. The daylight was as fuzzy as my head. I showered in cold water, hoping to clear my mind of the snarl that clogged the routes along which sanity traveled. Even black coffee lacked something. When the time came to leave, my crew was not welcome to ride in the large black SUV that delivered me to the St. John's lockup. It would be better if they remained aboard and got to the bottom of the steering problem. At least that's what I said, with no conviction. As I gazed out the car window, a faded tapestry of the city of St. John's rolled by in muted color and sound. We came to a stop. I was led from the vehicle to the back entrance of my destination, where garbage cans and loading docks crowded. One of my escorts pressed buttons on a phone and seemed to talk in code. Two new badges and holstered guns appeared and took possession of me. We wove our way through a labyrinth of corridors and stairwells until a door opened revealing a brightly lit room where the processing took place.

And that's how I landed in jail.

The sound of the cell door slamming closed was a wake-up call of startling magnitude. The cold-shower head clearing and black-coffee caffeine pumping hadn't cleared the fog, but in one moment reality came flying to the surface as the outside world was shut away. With neither nautical miles gone or to go, nor number of fish to tally, I had no way to mark time. My only method of measurement was the beating of my own pulse. As that got wearisome, I gave up the count at what I figured was close to three hours.

My attorney eventually joined me in my cell and explained

that we would soon go before the judge. He left, and I waited. After what seemed an eternity of practicing what I would say to the judge, I was handcuffed and taken from my cell by two female police officers. (The fact that I'm referring to the space as "my cell" is the only indication of how long I was actually detained—long enough to assume ownership.) The women were nice, I thought, to ask whether I preferred to be cuffed behind my back or in front of my waist, although "nice" was an adjective that could be relative. With no hesitation to hint at inexperience, I chose behind my back. *Click, click,* and it was done.

Just like in the movies, I was led with an officer on each side, all of us seemingly connected at our elbows, through long, dark hallways. It was unnervingly quiet but for the echoes from our footsteps, until we approached a gathering of people who hushed as we squeezed through. Some of them aimed cameras topped with stingingly bright lights at my face, making it difficult to see. I searched the crowd through squinted eyes and was overwhelmed with relief when I caught a glimpse of Archie. Brief eye contact supplied a more solid connection than any spliced line could. I knew that Archie was there, and he saw that I was okay. Nothing else mattered. He had ignored my order to remain aboard the *Seahawk*—and not a day has passed when I haven't been thankful for that.

My hands were freed from the cuffs before I entered the courtroom. I was shown a seat in front of a full audience and sat facing the judge. My attorney was there, as well as another man in a suit and tie who I knew must be the prosecutor. Some legal mumbo jumbo spoken in a Newfoundland brogue that I heard but did not comprehend was followed by the judge's asking me if I understood the charges. I hesitated. The judge clearly stated the charges as (1) illegal entry into Canadian fishing zone and (2) illegal fishing in Canadian fishing zone. "Yes, I understand the charges" was all I got out before the judge dismissed me from his courtroom. I didn't even get a chance to say "But—" before I was cuffed and whisked away to my cell to wait for the proper paperwork to be completed so that I could be released. The judge had given permission for my attorney to represent me at arraignment, which was just about the extent of what transpired.

I was furious. But time spent alone in my cell covered the pot and saw the boil reduce to a simmer. I couldn't believe I had just experienced my anticipated "day in court." It was all over without any opportunity to defend, deny, explain, or throw myself on the mercy of the institution. I didn't know what an arraignment was, nor did I care. I just wanted to jump aboard the *Shithawk* and get back to business. Wasting time fed more pissed-offness to my already pissed-off self. But all I could do was sit and stew in my own juices, as they say. I wished I had a cellmate to bitch to. I paced the floor.

The little peephole in the door slid aside, exposing half a face. The cell door swung open, and my attorney said that I was free to go now. It could have been hours or days for all I knew. He said that someone was waiting for me with a car, and asked that I follow him. He warned that there would be media burning film and asking for comments. He advised that I not comment. The processing officers bade me adieu with smiling faces. The cameras had thinned out, with only a few hangers-on left to record me reclaiming my freedom. Apparently a handcuffed female American captain being led into captivity was more newsworthy than one exiting on her own steam. Someone did ask if I had anything to say. I answered,

"No, thank you," and wished the attorney hadn't been with me. I knew I had the ability and ammunition to put real teeth in sound bites. Oh, well, I still had an arraignment in three weeks and, I supposed, a trial. For the first time in twenty-five years, I regretted not following my mother's advice to go to law school.

The status of being freshly sprung from jail did not evoke the feelings that I'd assumed it would. Freedom just did not live up to its hype. Not that I wasn't happy to see Archie and Jim Budi, but I still felt burdened. Arch gave me a bear hug and wiped a tear from the corner of his eye. "It nearly killed me to see you in handcuffs. I wished that I'd been the one arrested," he said. And I knew he was sincere. Jim drove while he and Arch filled me in on what was happening back aboard the boat and among the fleet. The electric motor that was responsible for the *Seahawk*'s steering had been examined and condemned. The other crews were finding their own lousy luck. One of Scotty's men had broken a wrist, putting an abrupt end to their fishing in order to take him ashore. (Oh, good, I thought, then reprimanded myself for being so petty.) And among our own crew, Dave Hiltz was suffering from kidney stones and was slated to go home. By the time the motor could be replaced, a new man could be flown in to take over for Hiltz. And the fish were biting. An electronics man was working on some of the faulty equipment and would remain on the job, fixing whatever he could until we sailed. And the fish were biting. Arch had lined up a guy to replace Hiltz. He had booked a ticket from Florida and would arrive tomorrow night. And the fish were biting. Scotty had to come ashore, and I wasn't able to get out and take advantage of a head start. I couldn't help but think I might as well have stayed in jail another twenty-four hours—even if the fish were biting.

The layer of the onion that I found most distasteful was losing Hiltz. I was so happy with the team I'd assembled; I doubted the unit could be as strong without my friend Dave. I never have been really at home with complications that arise on land. Too many years of coping with things at sea, where the options are few, if any, had spoiled me for contending with problems on the high and dry, where there are many possible resolutions. If Hiltz had had kidney stones offshore, he would suffer until he passed them. But here we are. And if it's Dave's prerogative to opt out, then far be it from me to ask him to buck up. I had worked with crew members who'd been so sick for so long that I thought they might die before we made landfall. But I'd never cut a trip short because of it. I didn't know much about kidney stones, but I had never heard of anyone dying from them. I couldn't wait to throw the lines. The fish were biting.

We pulled up beside the *Seahawk*. Hiltz was sort of hunched over the fish hold's hatch with a gallon of water in one hand and rubbing his lower abdomen with the other. I hopped out of the car and stepped aboard. "Gee, that didn't take as long as I thought it would," Hiltz said. He grimaced. His usual high color had turned pale.

"Really?" I asked. "You're kidding, right? It sure felt like a long time to me."

"Try this for a while."

"No, thanks. I'd rather be incarcerated, handcuffed, humiliated, and gain a criminal record that will tarnish my otherwise perfect reputation for life than pass a grain of sand through my weenie."

"It fuckin' hurts."

"I'll bet it does. So you're going home?"

"I don't think I have any choice. I hate to desert you like this. I'm really sorry."

Before I could further my efforts to sway a change of heart in Dave, thinking that he was using the stone as an excuse to bug out of the snowballing calamity I called a fishing trip, Timmy appeared on deck carrying the electric motor. It was large and looked extremely heavy. I couldn't imagine how any one man could have managed to lug it up from the engine room. The guy was a brute, plain and simple. His massive forearms were streaked with grease and rust, and sweat ran the length of his face and dripped from his chin. He placed the fried motor gently on the deck and said, "Here's the culprit." Then, as an afterthought, he added, "The motor—not you, Linda." Timmy's signature grin was infectious and elicited the same from me in return, one I knew was the first in some time. "I'm sure glad to see you. I hope it wasn't too bad."

Out from the galley waltzed Machado with an overstuffed sandwich. He bore the telltale signs of having assisted Timmy in the engine room; both perspiration and grime stained his sleeveless T-shirt. "Hey, Linny! You're out, thank God. How bad was it?" He extended the paper plate, offering me some of his sandwich. I gladly accepted half, sat on the hatch, and replayed my experience to the guys, perhaps exaggerating slightly the tightness of the cuffs and the time endured in them. My men had been working aboard the boat while I was in jail. This was certainly a switch. I entertained them for a few minutes. Then we got to the important part: How soon could we get back offshore?

Timmy and Arch ran down what they understood of our schedule. Today was Friday, they explained, as if I had just come out of a time capsule. The new steering motor would be installed tomor-

row morning, and Hiltz's replacement would arrive at ten tomorrow night. It would not be possible to leave the dock any earlier
than midnight tomorrow. So, they reasoned, there was plenty of
time for the electronics man to repair some of the primary equipment essential to our fishing success and safety and for us to enjoy
a bit of St. John's. Machado chimed in here with a recommendation
that we check out George Street, which I knew from experience
was Newfoundland's answer to Bourbon Street in New Orleans.
Fishermen on George Street? Bad news as far as I was concerned. I
thought back to the many nightmarish results of evenings spent on
George Street by various members of my crew. I doubted that the
street famous for the number of drinking establishments and foot-
loose, fancy-free women had aged at the same pace I had. But, I
wondered, who was I to restrict or advise? I suggested that we all
work aboard until dinnertime, have a meal out together, and then
go our separate ways, mine being straight to bed.

And that's exactly what we did. Dinner was excellent, although
I was a bit preoccupied with fears of what kind of trouble the men
might find after I retired and left them to their own devices, and
I worried about our timing in relation to the moon and the best
fishing, and the sad fact that I was not in a position to take advantage of Scotty's misfortune. Hiltz pulled himself together long
enough to eat, but he was clearly in some pain and quite willing
to head back to the *Seahawk* with me rather than venture out
with his shipmates. Arch and Tim both decided to call it a night,
too, leaving Machado to wander George Street alone. Arch was
tired, and Hiltz didn't feel well enough to carouse about. This was
the weirdest bunch of guys I had ever sailed with. Timmy didn't
drink. Not as part of a rehab or a twelve-step program; the man

did not drink, period. He had never even sipped a beer in his life, making him the most unlikely of my unlikely fishing crew. With 106 bars within walking distance of the boat, St. John's didn't have much to offer teetotalers in the way of nightlife.

The next morning I woke with the delighted realization that today was sailing day. We would be off the dock and headed for fishing before the stroke of midnight. All this trouble and nonsense of my arrest would be left behind, to be dealt with at a later date. The guys, except Machado, were up, drinking coffee and planning their day. We had a lot of work to do, but there would be a bit of free time this afternoon to relax and regroup for what we anticipated would be a long stint at sea. We all got busy, even Hiltz, who suffered through building new leaders while consuming as much water as he could in an attempt to flush the stone from his system before boarding his flight home the following day.

I drifted around, up and down from engine room to wheelhouse, and supervised a bunch of projects and chores that were being done by a combination of crew and hired professionals. The uneasiness of being ashore when others are catching fish was relieved in increments as jobs were completed and the time grew nigh for Air Canada to deliver my new man. Machado surfaced from his cavelike stateroom, perhaps a little hungover but cheerful enough. He regaled us with escapades that had ended at 3:00 A.M., which, surprisingly, did not include any women. His only acquaintance of the night was a homeless indigent named Brian, who enjoyed being treated to cocktails and a late-night snack. The recapping of his time with Brian reinforced what I was learning of Machado's kind soul shining through a gruff (and thick) exterior. He even had a picture of the cowboy-hatted Brian that he'd taken with his cell phone. "How'd you get rid of him?" I asked, sort of wondering if Brian was hiding somewhere with intentions of making a surprise appearance after we left the dock. (Hey, I've seen it all. Nothing is too outlandish to question.)

Machado knew what I was getting at. He laughed and said, "Don't worry. I poured him into a cab with a twenty. He's probably still touring the city." I relayed that I was overly anxious about leaving the dock and once again starting this trip. And Machado agreed that the time had come for our luck to change. He had enjoyed St. John's but was ready to go fishing. We all were.

The waiting was painful for me. I was ill at ease and out of sorts by the time the guys had finished their projects and were getting cleaned up. The electronics man had failed to actually fix anything. I set the men's curfew at 10:00 P.M. and reluctantly agreed that we were in no worse shape than when we'd left Fairhaven. The plan was to do whatever we wanted or needed until Jim Budi delivered our new man from the airport, which would likely be around 11:00 P.M. I was nervous about the guys leaving the boat, and I hoped they would return sober enough to throw the lines by midnight. Even though Tim had never had a drink, there'd been a first time for all of us. And some of us had had our first in St. John's. The locals call it "screeching in," for the rotgut rum distilled here. I had been nineteen, and never so sick in my life. That fear quickly dissipated when I learned that Tim and Machado were heading to a museum and Hiltz and Arch had planned an evening at an Internet café. I was so accustomed to digging my crew out of barrooms at sailing time that I found it hard to believe their plans did not include copious amounts of alcohol consumed in the spirit of "We may never pass this way again." Although I was getting to know and trust these men more and more, the bad experiences of the past were so pervasive and had been repeated so often that it was impossible to scour them from memory.

Arch insisted I join him and Hiltz at the café, where I could use his computer to touch base with everyone at home one last time. That was a brilliant idea, I thought. Ten years spent on or near shore had created ties to people other than shipmates, and ties meant certain responsibilities. I hadn't really given my parents the full story of why I was in Newfoundland. Now that I was out of jail, I could fill them in without worrying them as much as news of my arrest would have. I should also e-mail Sarai and see how school was going and assure her that I would indeed be home by Thanksgiving. Of course, I was sure I was the furthest thing from her mind, which I considered proper. But I was for all intents and purposes her parent, and I wanted to be responsible and acknowledge that I cared about her well-being. And Simon would naturally be interested in whatever I had going on that I hadn't already told him on the phone, which was nothing. But I would send him a note, too. Much better to occupy the last few hours doing something other than sitting and fretting. We all agreed to rendezvous for an early dinner, and off we went.

We had been in the café long enough for me to have finished three lattes when Archie decided to give his friend a call to let him know that Jim Budi would meet him at the airport and drive him to the *Seahawk*, where we would be waiting with the engine running. It was time for his layover in Newark, Arch said, and dialed the number. I didn't pay much attention to the conversation, as I was deep in a phone call with my mother—filling her in on the details of my arrest, including my opinion that I hadn't done anything wrong and that everything would work out as soon as I had my day in court, and also getting all of the latest scoop from home. I finished with my mother, promising that I would call next when I returned to Newfoundland to unload a whopping catch— I guessed that would be in three weeks or so. When I hung up, I saw that both Arch and Hiltz were staring at me. "What?"

"I got him. He's still in Florida. He says he thought he needed to be here *tomorrow* night," Arch said with an air of disgust.

"Are you friggin' kidding me? We're not staying here another twenty-four hours," I said. I thought for a few seconds before adding, "Call him back and tell him not to bother boarding the flight. We'll go shorthanded." And I meant it. My desire to cast the lines had increased to a desperate need. That need had tentacles that stretched and wound and tightened to a strength that threatened to choke me with the possibility that we would remain in Newfoundland while others were catching fish. It wasn't inconceivable that Scotty might beat me to the grounds (again) while I sat wasting precious time. "Come on, let's get out of here and find Machado and Timmy."

Hiltz stood and said, "I've passed these things before. I'll be fine. Let's go catch some fish." So Hiltz had done the right thing. I knew he would. It was near time to meet the others for dinner. The three of us hustled to the prearranged rendezvous, with me leading the charge powered by an inkling that if I hesitated for a split second, something would change and we'd be stuck here forever.

We met. We sat. We explained. We ate. We threw lines from the dock with a flourish and attitude that the third time was the charm. My grip on the gearshift as I pushed it forward was real. The transformation from out of body to here and now was spontaneous. As I steered the *Seahawk* through the sheer-faced cliffs that protect the port, I felt deliciously exposed. Leaning with both elbows on the window ledge, hands propping up my chin, I stared down Newfoundland. Not blinking was, for me, a small yet palpable victory in a sea of seemingly random defeats. I stood firm as the Canadian province grew smaller and smaller in the center of my view, looking aft. Dark evergreens merged with grizzled gray bluffs until their blurred amalgamation was surrounded in swirling blues of sky and water—like a stubborn clot in settled-out paint, freshly stirred. The slow-motion shutter that narrowed the lens eventually closed tight, relieving me from the eye-watering contest. The effect of distance was better for the eyes than for the soul. "Out of sight, out of mind" was just an expression with no credibility, I thought sadly. Newfoundland was gone. But not so the feelings that lingered.

The judge had agreed to allow my attorney to represent me at the arraignment on October 27. That was good news, as I expected to be in the midst of finishing up a trip at that time, or at least attempting to put some weight on the boat. The fish that we'd caught in our first, only, and ill-fated set were in the hold—all whopping twelve of them. Of course, their presence only added to the irritation that I was now finding difficult to abandon in our wake. As far as I knew, whenever a vessel was charged with illegal entry and/or fishing in Canadian waters, its catch was seized and sold by the officials, as it was considered to be the property of Canada. In my case the authorities could find no market in St. John's for swordfish. Thus I retained ownership of the contraband fish. In my opinion it wasn't as if I had inadvertently taken some-

thing from Canada that they wanted or valued in any way. I had
never known of any swordfishing boats that hailed from Newfoundland. There were some vessels that fished out of Nova Scotia. But they export all their catch to the United States, effectively
driving down the price that Americans receive as nonrecipients
of the generous government subsidies guaranteed to Canadians
by their keepers. It wasn't as if I'd been fishing for their sacred
cod, which had always been tantamount to stealing bread and
butter from the very mouths of hungry Canadian children. As it
turns out, you can't *give* swordfish away in Newfy. I'd accidentally
taken something from them that they didn't even want.

I reluctantly tossed the bucketful of sour thoughts over the
stern and turned back to again face the bow. Consciously refrain-
ing from taking one last look over my shoulder, I knew it was time
to stop thinking like a scolded child and begin thinking like a
fish. Much of the success of this trip, if there was to be any degree
of triumph, would be due to some entry into the psyche of my
lifelong adversary, *Xiphias gladius*, broadbill, or the almighty
sword. With 260 miles to go to the fishing grounds, or roughly a
day and a half, there wasn't an abundance of time to reintroduce
myself to the thought process and the philosophies I'd spent so
many years developing in the pursuit and capture of the target
species.

The Sea Shepherd Conservation Society's published description of me, which Archie had run across while surfing the Net, as
the "Notorious Serial Swordfish Killer" echoed in the recesses of
my short-term memory. The title wasn't actually haunting, but it
was distracting in its unfairness. Is that what people who don't
know me really think? I wondered. I had never thought of myself

as a murderer, even on my best day of fishing. I'd never had a lust for watching the life be decanted from a carcass. Nor had I acquired a taste for blood. Whatever killer instinct had existed in me, I suspected, had been driven by hunger. It had always been a situation of catch fish or fail, catch fish or don't eat, catch fish or don't get another chance—lose the boat, lose the crew. In the past I *had* to kill fish. It was a matter of survival in the business that had become my life. Any loss of hunger would be compensated for by passion. I love the hunt, the battle, and the conquest. These passions had not dulled.

I was headed back offshore. I was headed to where I would struggle against entities larger than what hides behind a badge or legal jargon. I would face real, meaningful challenges in a world that—although unpredictable and unstable—makes sense to me. I was headed to a world I understand, where kidney stones are like hangnails. If it's not life-threatening, it's not worth mentioning. Sure, I would be back in beautiful Newfoundland to unload a trip of fish. But it would be on my own terms. Home is a feeling more than a residence. And I was headed there.

CHAPTER 12

Back to Business

D arkness waded in cautiously and headed west. Hesitat-
ing waist-deep, then plunging into the murky chill, the
diving night splashed light onto the opposite horizon,
which swam like spawning salmon up the riverlike sky. The sun
hatched as if it were a baby chick, pecking from within the shell
until fully risen, yellow and warm, and as unsure as I was. Quite a
grand entrance, I thought enviously. After all, the sun starts anew
every day. This could well be my last chance. This was it. And I
would make the most of it. There would be no more practice runs
or dress rehearsals. If I couldn't make a go of it this trip, starting
today, swordfishing would become a dog-eared, stinking page
torn from my life's binding. I'd crumple it up, toss it over my
shoulder, and go on. Suddenly in my mind's eye, I dove and caught
the paper ball before it hit the ground. Jesus! What was I thinking?

I lovingly smoothed the page and tucked it close to my heart. It would be a hell of a lot easier to succeed.

I had my own recipe for success, tested and time-proven. The main ingredient was work, plain and simple. I had always believed that a successful operation aboard a commercial boat would be the perfect business model for any enterprise. Not that I had experience in any other—my résumé is short: I fish and I write about fishing. But I do have a sense of corporate America, large and small, that leads me to say that commercial fishing is exactly like any other moneymaking endeavor. Every fisherman is an entrepreneur of sorts in his risk taking and initiatives. And, in the same vein, I suppose the members of my crew are freelancers, hired on for the trip or season. Of course, the captain is much like a middle manager, juggling pins between owner and underlings. All the worn-out, clichéd crap about business management—like teamwork and leadership—top the priority list aboard a boat. But it would be all the subtleties of leading and working together that would make the difference in this business venture. This team I had assembled had a certain synergy I was confident could overcome any of the usual challenges and obstacles that would come our way. Yes, it was time to get down to the *business* of fishing.

A fitting symbol for my profession is the treble hook. Like Neptune's trident, commercial fishing is a three-pronged entity. The most obvious aspect of the three is in the physical realm. The physical part was the easiest for me. It's manual labor. It's the part I had always felt best suited for. With persistence and determination, I had been able to bull my way through any physicality. Fighting the elements of time, tide, weather, mechanical problems, fatigue due to sleep deprivation, and the basic moves involved in the daily operation of setting, hauling, and handling fish could be explained or taught in a book accompanied by a DVD, if such material existed.

Success on the physical level would not be possible without successfully meeting the second of the three elements—the psychological/emotional challenges. There are certain emotional facets inherent in going and staying offshore for extended periods, away from home and loved ones and the mainstream of life as the rest of the world sees it. I conquered those long ago but worried that my crew might struggle. The only cure for homesickness is going home. And going home would not be on the agenda for some time. On the psychological side, the challenges are twofold: shipmates and competition. Although I can get along with just about anyone, I've worked with men who have tested that capacity. Occasionally there are two men aboard a boat who dislike each other with an intensity that leads to fistfights. My cure for that has always been to levy fines. The threat of losing pay has never failed to lengthen short tempers. I could foresee no problems among my present crew, leaving lots of room in my head for the contemplation of jousting with my counterparts captaining other vessels.

Jockeying for position with a real strategy, holding that position once gained, and balancing ethics with competition could only be learned from experience. I could jockey with the best of them. I believed that the strategy for successful fishing hadn't changed, as swordfish themselves hadn't evolved noticeably during my ten-year sabbatical. Fishermen certainly hadn't changed—everyone wants to catch the most, the fastest. There would be sandbagging and exaggerating. There would be out-and-out lies. I had heard and told my share. Finagling and manipulating were important in this business, as I assume they would be in any business, maritime or not. There is nothing malicious in this form of deceit. It's expected. There are rules of engagement to be followed. For example, the first captain to drive stakes (so to speak) from a certain latitude and longitude to another latitude and longitude claims that berth, or span of ocean, in which to set his gear. He owns that berth until he gives it up. Ethical fishermen follow the unwritten rules. Simply stated, it's first come, first served.

On the most rudimentary level, he with the most fish wins the competition. But he with the most fish does not always make the most money. There's real strategy involved in hitting the market with fish at the right time to receive the highest price, and that competition brings with it another layer of deceit. It serves the paycheck well to land fish when the rest of the fleet is still fishing or steaming, even if it means cutting your trip short to get the big price. Of course, we also compete for price with imports from Canada, Chile, Spain, and several other places whose fishermen are not held to the same standards of conservation that U.S. swordfishermen are. Nothing cuts deeper than the news that Canada has just dumped fish on your market after you've left the fishing grounds and lost your berth to another boat while trying to slink away and beat the fleet to the dock.

The third prong in this business of fishing is more obscure. It's difficult to articulate, but I think of it as conquering "the fishing ocean" as opposed to the physical ocean. The fishing ocean is never a level playing field but is at least consistent in its unpredictability. Sure, I can calculate drift and find thermoclines. I can place gear in water that birds seem to like and that color and tem-

perature indicate fish will, too. But the fishing ocean is less ex-
plicit. It can be, in its most profound moments, esoteric to the point
of being devious. All the physical signs can be heart-poundingly
perfect, sirens luring me to set gear only to find nobody home. I
suspect that success on this level, however vague, would be considered having "business sense" or some innate ability. There is
no Fishing Made Easy course that can teach this part. Either you
have it or you don't. I used to have it. But I did always wonder if I
really had some gift or whether my success was more of an ability
to compensate for the lack of it with sheer work ethic. Whichever
the case, I understood my business of fishing and was ready to
engage.

I knew from experience that success today aboard the *Sea-*
hawk hinged on our ability to conduct business simultaneously
and seamlessly in these three aspects. We would face skirmishes
on all fronts, each of which would call for its own kind of intensity and expertise to overcome. If I think of myself as the CEO,
my success will be facilitated by my ability to get the most from
my employees. In my experience the way to do that was to lead by
example. Commanding a crew is more about inspiring them to
diligence and competence than it is about actual commanding.
Merely barking orders doesn't achieve desired results for me. I
work *with* my crew. They do not work *for* me. Respect is earned
and cannot be demanded. Competition is fierce. Desire had been
thwarted until now. When heart and soul went in, something
would come out. Ethics would be tested.

As we neared the grounds, sparsely populated by the remain-
ders of the dwindling fleet, I wondered if my nautical education
would serve me as well now as earlier. Had I missed some lesson

critical to success? I'd been a student of the business of being on the ocean all my life. My classroom had been tidal pools, clam flats, and the decks and bridges of boats. I had completed incidental courses in meteorology, oceanography, marine biology, navigation, mechanics, psychology, sociology, religion, and some very hard lessons in economics. Sure, my education was ongoing. I just hoped the Grand Banks curriculum hadn't changed.

Any apprehension I felt about competing on the water was displaced with the comfort of knowing that I had the ability to define my own standard for winning. Like the commercial fishing business itself, success within it was also threefold. The completion of a trip "from dock to dock," as we say, regardless of fish caught and hence money made, is a successful trip. Simply getting off the dock and back to it in one piece is often not so simple. Seamanship, or a captain's seaworthiness, is a combination of equal parts experience and common sense. I had to believe that I possessed bigger portions of both at the age of forty-seven than I had at thirty-eight. A second dimension of success, and the yardstick held by most people, would be to measure the success of any given trip by how full the hold is and not so much by the bottom line, as we have no control over the price of fish. Third, there's my old standby, the one that never fails—the feeling of fulfillment that comes when life and livelihood join forces in work you love.

The wind was blowing out of the east, and the sea had built to a steep chop. The *Seahawk* pounded through, rather than riding up and over the waves, sending rivers of green water along either side of the deck that spread and poured out of the scuppers and off the stern like spilled milk from a tilted table. Our progress to the grounds had slowed accordingly, and it was now apparent that setting gear this evening was questionable. *Not* fishing was the epitome of the anticlimax. Just one more delay. Everything was all prepped and set up to go. The crew was waiting for the word to get some bait out of the freezer. The GPS now indicated that at our present speed we would arrive at the general area where the five swordboats currently working on trips were situated at 11:00 P.M. That was not too late to set if we were dialed in on a spot and had been fishing it. But I would need some time to do the usual scoping out and lining up with the other guys, so I could get into the best spot without actually encroaching on someone else's hard-earned turf. By the time we had pounded our way to within striking distance, it had become clear that none of the other boats were setting gear, due to the weather conditions and the forecast for the following morning. Paradoxically, this bit of news caused an instant and palpable rush of excitement in me.

"Hey, Arch!" I yelled down the stairs. "Get the guys up! Thaw enough bait for eight hundred hooks!" Archie responded quickly and enthusiastically. As long as nobody else was fishing, I wouldn't worry about where I set. I'd steam to the best berth and at least get a night's fishing in while the competition sat it out. I wouldn't tell anyone that we were setting until the gear was in the water. If I announced now that I intended to set, it would force everyone to fish. Nobody wanted to look like a wimp. And, more important, nobody wanted to put out the welcome mat at the front door of his piece of water. The weather wasn't *that* bad, I justified. Even though there were few boats in the area, they had narrowed down the zone to fish by trial and error and were somewhat jammed up around where the Gulf Stream makes a bend from north to east. This corner of the stream where the current changes direction ninety degrees was always my favorite spot to fish, as it was nearly always the most productive. The other captains would be sound asleep and resting up for tomorrow night by the time I began my set. No sense waking anyone up. I now had a golden opportunity to slip into the high-liners' berth. This was not a new trick by any means. In fact, I had learned about it from the receiving end.

As we continued to thrash about in the ever-increasing waves, our pace now at a virtual crawl, I remembered that frustrating business lesson with not-so-fond feelings. I was captain of the *Gloria Dawn* at the time, my first boat, and was in the midst of what was becoming a prolonged trip northeast of the Flemish Cap (another twenty-four hours to seaward than our present position). Fifteen sets into what my crew and I had been enduring in the way of weather—bad enough to provide us with a real physical beating, making everything more difficult than usual yet not bad enough to warrant a night off—I finally relented and decided to keep the gear aboard due to a prediction of worsening conditions. The fishing hadn't been spectacular. In fact, we were in the process of setting a perfect example of grinding away and hoping for improvement, or at least high prices for what we were catching. We had enough bait and fuel for another four sets, and the moon was on the rise. Nothing but benefit could come from a night off at this point. We all needed a night's sleep. The moon needed to grow. The weather needed to straighten out. And the fish needed to get hungry.

There were at least forty boats strung along the break from the west side of the tail of the Grand Banks, around the southern tip, and up the east side all the way to well east of my position at about midfleet. My berth had not been producing anything more than what the others were reporting, but I was aware of the potential of this particular spot. When the fishing turned on, this would be the best of it, and we could very well put a slammer trip aboard in a couple of nights. As I now recalled, about half the boats made the same decision that night, with the other half fishing to keep tabs on what was what. The next night we'd switch. It was a real concerted effort and coordinated agreement to increase everyone's productivity while sparing valuable bait and fuel during this period of slow fishing. It's a known fact that fishermen always cooperate and work together for the good of all when the fishing is lousy. When the fish are biting, it's every man for himself.

I slept soundly that night so many years ago aboard the *Gloria Dawn*. It was the first time I'd had more than a short nap in two weeks. I woke before daylight with the realization that the weatherman had been wrong. The wind had dropped out, and I instantly regretted being included in the nonfishing half of the fleet. When I entered the wheelhouse to take over the watch just before dawn, I could see the lights of another vessel off in the distance. I cranked the radar to a range that showed the boat at eight miles from me. I hadn't seen another vessel since we'd begun fishing this trip, as we were all setting end to end and no one had been inside or outside my forty-mile slot. I grabbed the VHF's microphone and hailed the boat eight miles southwest of me. The reply was immediate. "Hello, Linda! It's Captain Tommy on the *Miss Leslie*."

Oh, no, I thought. Tommy was the clown of the fleet in his total ineptitude. Nobody wanted to fish near Tommy. I knew I had to drive him away by whatever means it took. Tommy was a complete menace. He once set forty miles, hook for hook, right on top of another man's gear, and his boat broke down before they had the mess straightened out, forcing the other captain to haul both strings and take the idiot under tow. Tommy just always screwed things up. Stupid like a fox, he always pretended not to understand where he was or where he needed to not be, and he had always been suspected of hauling other people's gear and stealing fish. Tommy was famous for doing whatever he wanted, where he wanted, regardless of whom he was stepping on, then later begging for forgiveness for his honest mistake. I hadn't heard Tommy on the radio since I'd started this trip, so I knew he was probably just arriving and looking for a spot. "Hi, Tommy. You must be headed to the east end of the fleet. Jerry has been starting around the forty-one line. With this nice weather and favorable tide, you can make it to his east end in time to set out. Over."

"I don't know. We'll see what happens here today. I'm just getting ready to pick up my end buoy. Come in."

"End buoy? You've got gear in the water? Over," I asked as my stomach turned.

"Yep. I got it in late last night, but I think it looked pretty good. I'll let you know. Come in."

"*You'll* let *me* know? Tommy, you're in my berth. I'll be fishing here tonight. Over."

"Well, I heard you weren't fishing last night. I have to get busy here. Talk to you later. Bye." And he was gone. I was enraged. Tommy had just managed to sneak a set into a spot I'd fished for fourteen consecutive nights. If he caught any fish, it would be impossible to budge him. I prayed that he would have such poor fishing that even *he* would think he could do better elsewhere. I prayed that he would be all fouled up and not be able to get his gear back aboard in time to set again, and he'd drift into the next berth and be out of my way. I spent the day kicking myself. Late that afternoon Tommy was back on the radio with a report of ten fish. That was about half of what I'd been catching. But I didn't know whether he was telling the truth. I told him that I was getting ready to toss my end buoy and wished him well wherever he might be going. Tommy said that he would like to stay here and set alongside of my gear, as he knew I was nearing the end of my trip and he'd like to take over my berth when I left.

"I have bait for at least five more nights, Tommy. You might be better off finding your own set. The break has been too tight for two abreast. Over."

"It's too late for me to get anywhere else and set tonight. I'll try it next to you. What water temperature will you be favoring? Come in."

"I'll be working the whole break, from cold to hot. The fishing hasn't been good enough to fine-tune the set. And now that I've missed a night, things may have changed. I'll be covering all of the bases. I think you'd be better off finding your own berth. Over."

"I caught all ten of my fish on the warm side of the edge. So I'll fish outside of you. What time are you starting? Come in."

There was no shaking him off. I was stuck with the jerk. And I didn't trust him. If he said he wanted the warmer water, he might be tricking me into fishing warmer myself so he could have the cooler side of the break. On the other hand, he might realize that I didn't trust him and be trying a reverse con job on me. The only solution was for me to make my set the way I normally would but perhaps making sharper turns that Tommy couldn't possibly follow in and out, forcing him to stay well off my gear and, I hoped, out of the fish. But, I realized, Tommy might attempt to mirror my set and end up all over me, screwing both of us up and ensuring that neither of us caught anything the next day, since everyone knows that tangled gear does not fish.

I decided to start on the warm side of the break, not because Tommy wanted to be there but because that's just the way I wanted to fish my gear. Five miles into my set, Tommy called asking for my beeper numbers and water temps and positions at turns. He had changed his mind and was now setting on the cold, or inside, of my gear. I warned him that he might be in the sharks, because I planned to touch the cold on every pass over the temperature break, leaving him in ice water for much of his set. He didn't seem to care until the next day.

"Fuckin' blue dogs! I'll never get this shit back aboard! You can have this fuckin' spot all to yourself!" It was like music to my ears as I watched my crew clean and ice the last of the fifty-five fish we landed that day. And off to the east Tommy drifted, out of my berth and into the next in line, fouling up his new neighbor in good shape. All these years later, I could still feel the sense of relief.

I chuckled now as I watched the *Seahawk*'s water-temperature gauge climb quickly from fifty-six degrees to sixty-seven. Nice edge, I thought, and just below my favorite corner. I'd silently set here and drift right into the sweet spot before anyone was the wiser. From out of the darkness, a single renegade wave slammed the bow with force enough to send the boat back into the crest as it broke over the bow and flooded the deck. I watched out the back window as the crew scrambled around trying to catch the boxes of bait as they sloshed rail to rail in the knee-deep water. Wind-driven rain was pelting the side of the wheelhouse, sounding like a drumroll. Just a squall, I told myself. The next sea caught us on our port beam, rolling the boat onto her side so far that she dipped the end of the port outrigger. Crew and bait were pinned against the gunwale until she rolled back the other way, sending all cascading to the opposite side with the water. I pulled the throttle back. I thought about Tommy. I do not want to be that guy, I thought. I am not that desperate.

It's a woman's prerogative to change her mind. Safety, being the first concern, was now on edge and teetering, teasingly toeing the line. I opened the back door long enough to yell to Archie to wrestle the bait into the freezer again, then swung the boat around, putting the now-hefty seas on our stern, jogging fair wind just long enough for the guys to stow the bait and secure the deck for the night. We had enjoyed a great stretch of weather until now. We were due for a little blow. And here it was. "Better safe than sorry" had always been a successful motto. There was no sense adding to our previous roster of miseries by risking an injury. If someone did get hurt or the boat sustained some damage in this gale, it could be serious enough to cancel, rather than postpone, the entire effort. It was certainly wiser, and a better business decision, to knock the boat out of gear and drift with the fleet tonight.

The *Seahawk* rode up and over the waves like a duck with her starboard side to the wind. I was relieved to learn that the boat behaved so well lying to. With the rudder hard to port, the waves were pushing gently aft of amidships, each one landing a slightly glancing blow rather than slapping full on the beam. When I spread my bedroll onto the wheelhouse floor and hauled out my sleeping bag and pillow from under the chair, I estimated the wind velocity at around fifty knots. I was glad to have given my bunk to Timmy during my detour into St. John's, as it seemed so unfair for him to attempt sleep at the galley table. Someone was nearly always opening the fridge or turning on a light to make coffee. Besides, I'd always had my stateroom topside and felt it was the right place for the captain to be. I would certainly have preferred a bunk to the deck, since I hadn't found a comfy space that would allow my face not to be very close to the watch stander's feet. I tried at first to sleep on the chart table. But that required me to literally breathe down the neck of the man on watch. If I rolled over, my elbow stood a pretty fair chance of whacking in the head whoever was in the chair. And if the boat took a deep roll to starboard, I might just fly right off the table and shoot down the stairs. That combination of wickets became unnavigable after about two watches, which was when I hit the deck, so to speak. It was a bit of a frig to have to roll up the mattress and stow my bedding every morning, rather than just turn out of a bunk. Now the only danger was being stepped on. I liked being closer to what I needed to see and hear in order to perform the duties I expected of myself. So here I was on the floor and feeling okay about not setting.

I told my crew that I was putting our safety ahead of productivity on the priority list. And while this was true, it wasn't the whole truth. I would indeed have fished these weather and sea conditions if I hadn't been horning in on the *Destiny*'s berth. Billy had been at swordfishing a very long time and had no doubt experienced all the slimy moves and tricks that any pirate could pull from billowing sleeves. Billy was a savvy guy as well as a tough one. Payback would have come, and it would no doubt have rendered my slight misdeed not worth whatever it produced.

But fear of retaliation wasn't it either. Simply put, there is no joy in cheating. I love the process of fishing. Poaching, encroaching, stealing, interloping, pillaging—these had never been my way of conducting business. These illicit practices were reserved for people who fish solely for the money. I had learned long ago that if money is the prime motivator to go offshore, you're going for the wrong reason. Although I hadn't gone through with sneaking a set in, I did feel a tiny bit of shame for the adrenaline rush the prospect of doing so had created. There'd always been this hint of titillation in thinking bad thoughts about deeds I wouldn't carry out. I fell asleep that night watching the radar relentlessly sweeping its circular glass and knowing that I, too, was cleaning a slate of sorts.

Although the following day was a long one—waiting for five captains to wake up, waiting for five captains to make decisions about where they would begin setting, and waiting for five captains to estimate where they would finish their sets—we began our trip in earnest that night. We began it honestly and with integrity, in a slot just below Swanny, who was below Billy, who was west of Kenneth. A Nova Scotian by the name of Brett aboard the *Ivy Rose* arrived a bit late and strung his gear outside mine, leaving a nice wide, polite gap between the two strings. Scotty was closing in on the area and would be filling a space between Billy of the *Destiny* and Kenneth aboard the *Eyelander* the following night. Charlie Johnson, captain of the *Seneca*, and Barry Marx on the *Dee Cee* were steaming in and out respectively, so the fleet now consisted of five fishing and two traveling.

With so few boats, the ocean seemed to have grown, I thought as I wove back and forth across the temperature break from fifty-eight to sixty-five degrees. I was setting to the south and into the current, with intentions of steaming back to the north end of the gear to haul into the current the next day. Part of the business in this area is constantly stemming the tide, or working against it while setting and hauling, so as to hold ground and not drift away and out of the fleet and productive fishing. Tide is the one thing you can count on always working against you, making efficiency in hauling imperative. We can't stand for delays of any kind if we want to make sets back to back to back and put a trip aboard. I've had days when I won't even stop long enough to pose with a slammer sword for a quick photo.

I wasn't happy to see Archie on deck when he was supposed to sleep during set out so that he could steam the boat back to the other end while the rest of us slept. But I imagined he was too keyed up to miss the very first mark on our fresh slate. He caught me looking down from the deck behind the wheelhouse, flashed a big smile and a thumbs-up. "We're fishin', Linny!"

And we were indeed fishing. We were doing business! We managed to get the gear out and back and back out again without missing a beat. Of course, it's important to note that I've been known to be optimistic to the point of delusional. We were not revolutionizing the sword operation, but we were putting fish on the boat. Our first haulback tallied twenty-eight fish that averaged a little over a hundred pounds each, a very respectable start.

We were going through all the growing pains that are part of working a boat that has not been maintained to very high standards. Timmy, who had now proved himself invaluable in the engine room and on deck, was a real workhorse. He managed, with troubleshooting assistance from Archie, to keep everything belowdecks ticking. Because of the saltwater rain in the engine room, Timmy's daily maintenance was more extensive than what normally needs to be done aboard a vessel that doesn't have holes in the deck above the main engine. Timmy worked hard on deck, and even harder fixing run-down, derelict equipment. He took great pride in his work and smiled a lot when fielding frequent comments from the rest of us pertaining to his remarkable progress with the sow's ear. Not a day went by that I didn't get a report from Timmy: "I fixed it. I think we're okay now."

The biggest daily difficulties were the ratty main line and the beeper buoys. Archie, who was getting virtually no sleep, was plagued at night by the weak signals from the beepers as he attempted to steam the length of the gear without running it over. The lack of good beepers made for very long nights for Archie and me. Neither of us felt right about leaving the other to the totally frustrating task of trying to get the boat to the end buoy by daylight guided by signals that were faint at best and didn't indicate the correct direction until the buoy was within eyesight—totally defeating the purpose of the buoys. And part-offs were the worst. We were averaging three part-offs a day, with two days of five. Parted gear is time-consuming enough with good beepers. But with buoys that don't work well, they eat up days like nothing else, leaving us hauling gear way after dark on some occasions and later than everyone around us on all occasions. We didn't have as much main line as reported before we sailed. And we wouldn't have been able to fish any more than what we had in its poor condition. We didn't have enough floats to fish more than eight hundred hooks anyway. This put us at a distinct disadvantage in the friendly competition within the fleet of boats fishing, some of whom were running fifteen hundred hooks out the stern a night. But we were putting fish aboard.

Archie was a godsend. He was a nursemaid to the crew, dispensing Band-Aids, Dramamine, and fatherly advice. He really was the glue that kept the other guys together in spite of the hardships we hadn't anticipated. He put a hearty meal on the table every night. This is not an easy task in bad weather, but it's imperative for morale. I never knew when, or if, Archie slept. But if he did, it wasn't when I needed him to take a watch so that I could. I have a most vivid picture in mind of Archie with a cutting torch working on a bird-nested main-line spool that had suffered the worst backlash I'd ever seen. The drum had spun faster than the line was going into our wake while setting out night number six, creating a rather dangerous situation with loops of slack line going everywhere. Some of the loops jumped over the end plates of the drum, jamming tightly into the bearing. We had to terminate the set at three sections and spent the rest of the night clearing the spool of the messed-up line. Archie, who had finally decided to take a nap, came running onto the deck when he heard the boat slow down and worked in the cold rain and wind in bare feet until things were right. His sweatpants were so soaked they wouldn't stay up. Whoever had a free hand kept it on the back of Archie's waistband. Otherwise I'm sure he'd have worked bare-assed.

Hiltz was great, too. He had finally passed his kidney stone, an occurrence cheered by his shipmates, who were monitoring his visits to the head and who met each exit with, "Well?" Hiltz was sort of funny, with his short fuse. He would get disgusted, throw his hands in the air, and say, "That's it. I've had enough. I quit." The first time this happened, the guys were concerned. Hiltz took off his oil gear and went into the fo'c'sle, leaving us shorthanded on deck to finish hauling. He wasn't gone long, so I figured he was using the head. When he came back, he went right to work with a smile on his face as if he hadn't a care in the world. The quitting became a daily episode; he once quit three times in a single haul-back. In spite of the drama, Dave Hiltz was truly a great asset to our team. He absolutely did what he said he would when I hired him. He filled in and did what was needed when it was needed, assisting his shipmates in their duties, making himself the most willing and competent all-around crew member. Hiltz had taken full responsibility for the leaders, which required him to stay on deck even longer than the others to keep the boxes full of pristine gear. Hiltz was always the first guy with a gaff when a fish was alongside, and he was always quick to help in the fish hold. When we were catching sharks, Hiltz jumped in to relieve with the pulling of heavy leaders and releases. Machado even taught him to clean fish just in case he fell behind in a real flurry and needed help. Which brings me to Machado.

Mike Machado had an uncanny ability to tiptoe along a very thin line between being irreplaceable and being fired. By the time we'd completed a week of fishing, Machado and I were in a true love/hate relationship, as far as I was concerned. His whining and complaints were nonstop, ranging from a lengthy punch list of boat problems to issues with the groceries. He was an anomaly, one minute exhibiting sheer laziness, then just getting the job done, then doing it really right. Machado snacked while lying in his bunk. He got up one morning and found an entire Kit Kat bar in one of the folds of fat under his chin. When he ate the melted mess, I was torn between disgust and admiration. In job performance Machado was a great butcher, cleaning fish with speed and expertise. He also had the right rhythm in the stern of the *Seahawk* while setting out, baiting hooks, and keeping everyone entertained. But he dragged his feet every step of the way, no matter what we were doing. However, I must say that when the going was at its toughest, Machado always stepped up. He stepped up when I needed him most. He stepped up his physical game when he had to, and he always exploited his greatest asset—his sense of humor. I remember clearly a couple of instances when the chips were down—a combination of bad weather and poor fishing—and Machado regaled us all with monologues that would put certain late-night television hosts out of business.

I went to the galley one night expecting some long faces after a day of miserable weather and four part-offs that cost us this particular night's set. I was anticipating giving a little pep talk to the crew. The words of a former boss, Bob Brown, were ringing in my head as I descended the stairs: "We work on a share basis. We share the good, and we share the bad. Right now we're sharing the bad." Archie was putting food on the table as well as he could with the boat rocking and his eyes tearing from laughter. I had missed Machado's first act, so I caught his routine in midperformance. He was really getting on Archie about the menu. "Really, Arch, I'm not kidding. Gravy is not a food group, nor is it a staple of anyone's diet. Please tell me we have vegetables aboard. I mean, other than onions and potatoes. Come on, Arch. Where are the veggies? You know, the green stuff that grows in gardens? We *do* have some, don't we? Because I haven't seen any this trip. How about a salad? Did you order any lettuce? How about cabbage? I like coleslaw. We don't have a single veggie on board, do we? I'll have the first confirmed case of scurvy in the last century. My fuckin' teeth are rattling." And this from the guy who has treasure hunts for chocolate bars buried in his body parts.

"We have vegetables," Arch confirmed through a real deep stomach laugh. "In fact, we're having stuffing tonight. See?" And Arch set Machado's plate in front of him.

"Stove Top stuffing is not a vegetable, Arch. Jesus! Ronald Reagan told America that *ketchup* was a vegetable! He's responsible for an entire generation of malnutrition. Okay, forget about the green vegetables. Broccoli and spinach are apparently off the menu for the next forty days. But what about carrots? Or tomatoes? What the fuck? By the end of this trip, my teeth will have fallen out and I won't be able to chew a carrot anyway. Okay! Now I understand the abundance of cream-style corn aboard this fuckin' scurvy raft."

Arch held up the stuffing container, slipped his glasses from his forehead to the bridge of his nose, and read, "Celery, onions, parsley. That's green!"

"Onion *powder* and parsley *flakes*? You're trying to pass that shit off as vegetables? I never thought I'd be jonesing for asparagus. Linny, how's my complexion? I'm feeling weak and depressed. My gums are bleeding!" Now I was laughing so hard along with the crew that I couldn't answer. Not that Machado needed one. He kept going. The last I witnessed before taking my dinner topside was Machado holding the blue box of Morton kosher salt close to his cheek, caressing the picture of vegetables in the logo, and muttering, "Veggie porn, veggie porn."

Each time we had to miss a night of fishing because of late finishes in hauling due to part-offs and sick beeper buoys, we lost our place in the lineup with the fleet. But because we didn't set out, I had the next day to find a new berth—or search for greener pastures, as it were. The good nature of my crew only enhanced my attitude that the glass was barely one-quarter full. We had shifted positions a couple of times. It didn't seem to make much difference, as the fishing was just sort of average and we knew we needed to stick it out and keep grinding to put a trip on.

We were getting geared up for our eighth haulback when Archie couldn't pry Machado from the galley table without feeding him yet another pancake the size of a manhole cover. I was at the breaking point. I was on deck with Timmy and Hiltz and waiting for another warm body to begin hauling. The weather was foul, and I was already anticipating a long day when Machado finally graced the deck with his sauntering presence. The waves were building, and we took a sea that caused his dainty little foot to slip about an inch to one side from where he'd planted it while carefully donning his gloves. That was it. Machado went into one of his hissy fits, cursing the boat and its owner and declaring this whole scene a joke. He looked up at the sky, as if pleading with God to free him from his misery. "I'm a grown man! Why am I out here? I have a real job. This boat is sucking the life out of me!" The big guy was seriously frustrated. But I figured he'd work through it. He'd step up today. The weather was treacherous—the worst we'd seen yet—and we had thirty-two miles of gear to get aboard.

As I jogged up to the first beeper and attempted to get close enough for Hiltz to hurl the grapnel, we took one tremendous sea that flooded the deck and floated my platform so that I was now standing on a raft that was trying to go downriver. I held on and squinted into the wind-driven spray while the beeper came aboard. "Put the door in," I said, referring to the large wooden plate that closed the opening in the gunwale through which we pulled fish from the water and onto the deck.

"It doesn't fit! It gets stuck, and we'll never be able to get it out!" Timmy yelled, so he could be heard above the screeching wind. We took another sea that sent gallons of water directly down my neck, the length of my body, and into my boots. Great. I was already soaked, and we hadn't hauled a single hook aboard. This would be another fun-filled day on the *Shithawk*. My goal was to keep the boat on the gear and the gear coming aboard. I prayed for a day with no part-offs, which was like hoping for a miracle. As luck would have it, we caught two double markers right at the start. Two two-hundred-pound fish with the first five hooks! It was very exciting. The combination of fish and weather had the gear pretty snarled up, and we struggled to clear the mess. I was hustling in anticipation of the next fish and a big day. The gear is normally in one continuous line that zigs and zags but does not intersect itself. This first mile or so of this line looked like a doodle scrawled on a notepad after a very long, very boring meeting. The gear was everywhere. We had a major frig. And the weather didn't help.

I was in the middle of untangling three leaders that came up twisted together with our third fish, which had just broken the surface, when we got plowed by a wave that filled the entire workspace. The boat listed to port, and the water began to clear over the rail. All I could do was grab a steel post to avoid being swept overboard. I held on as the waist-deep water washed by me like a torrential undertow threatening to suck me away. I looked aft to check on the guys. I quickly counted four heads and went back to concentrating on holding on. Today's conditions would be the supreme test of my management skills. Head counts were something I guessed were unique to this industry. In other, landlocked careers, not punching a clock or missing a meeting was barely noticed. But here, being absent from deck was potentially tragic. Truancy in other jobs might lead to loss of pay or employment. A no-show after water clears aboard a commercial boat likely means loss of life.

Today I would have my hands full keeping the boat on the gear and the gear coming aboard the boat, and making sure the crew was all still on deck. This was the fishing business. We weren't doing a banner business. But we were fighting and succeeding in all aspects. Although we weren't yet the well-oiled machine I knew we would eventually be, we were making strides physically and meeting psychological challenges. Even the fishing ocean showed signs of succumbing to our charms.

CHAPTER 13

Shipping Seas

With all of this talk of managing, manipulating, and controlling, I would be remiss not to admit that fate also sits at the table with a fistful of cards. Managing Mother Nature is, of course, impossible. The best we can do in times of heavy weather and extreme sea conditions is to maintain that we are putting safety first, with the reality of knowing that we simply must retrieve whatever gear is in the water regardless of inherent danger. Unless the weather is so severe that I can't muscle the boat up to the end buoy to hook up to it in . . . let's say, three passes, we'll combat anything a low-pressure system can serve up until the last inch of line is spooled onto the drum. Preparing for the worst and hoping for the best is just not enough. Tossing arms in the air and giving in to what is conveniently deemed as fate or destiny is too easy. Although I preach personal responsibility and hold myself accountable for all that goes on aboard any vessel of which I'm in command, I have been made acutely aware of the role of what some might regard as the hand of God intervening at sea. The line between management and fate is somewhat equivocal and is always drawn subjectively in hindsight. This particular day, with ever-increasing wave height and wind velocity and deteriorating morale, my personal God seemed to have been having some fun at my expense.

Wind-driven spray had already left salty deposits in my eyelashes that scratched when I wiped them away with the back of a gloved hand. The best oil clothes money can buy are rendered useless when water seeks entry. My hood string was cinched as tight as I could get it without totally obstructing my vision or breathing. By the time we had half a section of gear aboard the boat, I was as soaked as if I'd just climbed out of a swimming pool. Gallons of water seeped down my neck and up my sleeves and pant legs, until my knee-high boots were full and running over, fountainlike. Cold wicked inward. There was no sense taking time to change into dry clothes, as they would only be drenched with the next inbound wave. Besides, I couldn't leave the deck and the controls in these elements when all hands were required to maintain some semblance of order in the hauling process. I was certain that every one of the guys was as wet and cold as I was, since water was just everywhere. Besides, none of my crew would be comfortable hauling the gear in these conditions even if I had the audacity to suggest it. So I accepted the fact that the five of us would be putting in another long, cold, wet day together.

The main line was still fouled up and showed no sign of

straightening, which made it difficult to get into the rhythm achieved when longline is hauled efficiently. There was no point in trying to hustle. Hurrying would only make things worse. We were catching fish, and retrieving the line too aggressively just enhanced the chances of losing fish from hooks if they were pulled too hard. "Pulling fish off" was something I prided myself on *not* doing—even at the expense of precious time spent going slowly and easily along. A hook coming aboard with nothing on it but a gill plate torn from a swordfish's face when gear was hauled in haste was something that the men in the stern were quick to point out. I had received many scolding, guilt-producing looks in the past and knew that today's weather conditions would result in an increased risk of pulling fish off as the boat helped yank the line when it surged up and down violently. Methodical patience was the order of the day.

Every time we shipped a sea, I turned to find the men clinging to whatever they could until the water from the wave crashing aboard had cleared enough for them to resume their various jobs. Machado was having the toughest time, as each rush of water over the deck floated the fish he was attempting to clean and stow before the next fish or next surge came aboard. The station where the fish were headed and gutted was the middle of the open deck. Machado had nothing to break a wave or to hang on to or to hide behind. He was not a real fun guy this morning. In fact, he was enraged and swearing at the top of his lungs about the situation in general while chasing runaway fish carcasses that rolled back and forth across the deck in the ever-sloshing nuisance water. While the rest of us found some humor in his act, he got madder and madder. As each sea retreated through the scuppers, Machado collected himself, his tools, and his victim just in time to be swatted down and scattered again. I hardly dared to be caught casting a glance toward him, for I knew from my years of working on deck that the captain is held responsible for all discomfort—whether it's justified or not. In spite of Machado's apparent unhappiness with our decent production, the rest of us joined in brief cheers between struggling to perform our duties and remaining in the positions required for us to do so. Things could be worse, I knew. We could be fighting the weather and *not* catching fish.

I pushed the *Seahawk*'s throttle up to wide open to swing her bow into the wind while another double marker was dragged onto the deck. As soon as the fish was safely aboard, I let the bow fall off, leaving the wind on our port side again, and I resumed the crawling pace along the serpentine gear. Just as I had the boat back on the gear properly, we took the worst wallop yet. Green water pounded the hull smack on our beam and cascaded like a giant waterfall over the rail. When the boat rolled to starboard, the volume of water collected and rushed that way, taking all that was in its path with it. My back was pressed securely against the side of the fo'c'sle, and I planted my feet to brace myself and avoid becoming part of the reaction. The boat rolled back to port, and the torrent buckled my knees briefly. I recovered and looked aft to see two fish slide toward the open door, followed closely by Machado, who was foundering flat on his belly and quite helpless.

The first fish went through the door and overboard. Machado's eyes were like saucers as he headed toward the opening through which the fish had just vanished. Although everything was happening at high speed, my memory of Machado is in slow motion. His arms and legs were spiraling much like the limbs of a turtle

stuck on its back and struggling to right itself, to no avail. Thinking back, I imagine Machado as an astronaut out of gravity's
grasp. Machado's expression was the perfect picture of sheer ter-
ror as he looked desperately for something to grab to save himself. A second fish splashed through the door that was now acting
as a funnel for the deluge of exiting water. There was no doubt in
my mind that Machado would immediately follow the fish. And
there wasn't a thing I could do to stop him. I threw the boat out of
gear to avoid moving away too quickly or chopping him up in the
propeller should the boat be blown down on top of him. I wondered if one of the guys could throw the life ring quickly and accurately enough. Suddenly, just as Machado's head went over the
threshold, Timmy appeared from out of nowhere. He dove onto
Machado, pinning him hard to the steel deck and stopping him
just short of being a goner.

It was quite a frightening scene. I had never lost a man overboard, and I understood that if one went in this weather, it would
be extremely difficult to get the boat close enough to him to pull
him back before he sank beneath the surface. My stomach turned
as I had a flash to the story of a man lost off the deck of the *Hannah Boden* and sinking from sight while the crew failed in attempts to harpoon him. I deliberately wiped from my mind the
image of Machado with a gaff hook in his head. If Machado had
been lost and not recovered, would fate be blamed? Or would I be
thrown under the bus for Mother Nature? Many a captain had
lost interest in the sea following a trip home absent one crew
member.

The water cleared. The boat stopped wallowing. I swung the
bow into the wind to allow everyone a second to regroup before

attempting to haul again. "Now, put that fucking door in!" I yelled at the top of my lungs. "I don't care if it never comes out. Didn't I say to put it in before we picked up the end buoy? This is not *my* first trip! Put the fucking door in!" I didn't mention that we had almost lost Machado. I didn't need to.

The big guy was clearly and understandably shaken by the near miss. I had no time to console him or do a psyche check—my job today was to keep the boat on the gear and the gear coming aboard. I eased back into hauling while Machado collected himself. Sawdust flew in the gale as Archie ground down the door so it would appropriately slide in and out of the slots that held it as needed. And we needed to remove it twenty-five times that day. Production-wise, it was our best day of the trip so far—I estimated a conservative three thousand pounds. If we could make another seven or eight sets, we would be going to the dock with a very respectable load. It was a super-long day, but a good one. We were still chasing part-offs after dark. All in a day's work, I thought with a shiver. I was mildly hypothermic and relieved to be hauling the last few hooks under a spotlight not quite bright enough to allow me to see the leaders coming. As the snaps ran into my fist, through which I allowed the line to run, I removed them mostly by feel and handed them to Archie, who'd been working faithfully at my side for the last sixteen agonizing, yet oddly satisfying, hours.

"I see the beeper," Arch said softly, referring to the welcome sight of the very end of the gear, marked by a strobe on the beeper's antenna that went in and out of view as it rode up onto a crest and down onto a trough. Seeing the end beeper after what we'd withstood today stirred emotion in the way I imagined hearing

"Land ho!" at the end of a very long voyage would have done a century ago.

"Just in the nick of time," I said with a smile.

"We were lucky to not lose Machado this morning," said Arch. No one had mentioned the incident all day, although I assumed that everyone was still thinking about it, as the image of a man so close to probable death was not one that would fade quickly. I hesitated and finally decided that too much time had elapsed for me to respond. Arch would think I hadn't heard him. I was the first to have a turn in the shower, and I stood with the hot water blasting the back of my neck. As the feeling came back into my fingertips, I couldn't help but contemplate Arch's opinion of our having been "lucky" to still have Machado aboard. Not that I would dispute the sentiment of Archie's statement—just the phrasing. I've always had trouble with the word "luck," even though I use it as often as other people do. Walking a line between believing that there are indeed things that can't be orchestrated or controlled and wanting to think that blame can only be placed on oneself in life makes for tough sledding when things go wrong. When events go against me, it's "the fickle finger of fate." When all is well, I'm a genius.

Our society in general has a need to place blame. This propensity to hold someone or something responsible for what could easily be explained as an act of God has never been as clear as it became in the months and years following the Halloween Gale of 1991, known now as the Perfect Storm. Once the American public learned all there was to know about the events that led to the deaths at sea of the six fishermen of the *Andrea Gail*, the questions began. Wasn't there a problem with the boat's stability? Isn't

it true that Bob Brown was a bastard? Wouldn't they have survived if the National Weather Service had accurately predicted
the storm? Do you think the captain made a mistake in steaming
directly into the storm? Why did he do that? The events of 1991
still intrigue and fascinate people. They often tell me I survived
that storm because I'm lucky. I beg to differ. I feel as though I did
everything right, and I attribute my survival to the seamanship
and skill of myself and my crew. If I believed that luck had a hand
in our survival, I would also have to believe that eventually our
luck would run out and I wouldn't dare go to sea ever again. It's
just too weird to believe that I'm alive simply because of fate and
that Billy Tyne and his crew are dead because someone screwed
up. Very few people are able or willing to shrug off ill fate as "bad
things happen." Someone must be at fault. It's just the way we
are. Having said all that, I'll add that there are no atheists at sea.
In times of peril, even the most stoic of seamen become quite
prayerful.

   Knowing and understanding the pervasive mind-set and the
need to point a finger didn't make me feel any better about today's
episode, which could have ended so badly. The general public
would never hear about our *almost* losing a man. They would
never hear about most of the daily heroics at sea. They wouldn't
know the bravery of Timmy. Or the mental strength and forti-
tude of my men and what they had endured today. They wouldn't
know the anguish and coping skills of men working and living
like animals, who are sometimes subject to fate. It's funny, I
thought as I sipped a cup of hot tea and watched the stars emerge
from a hole in the overcast darkness, I blamed myself for almost
losing Machado by not insisting that the door be placed in its slot,

closing the gaping hole, in spite of the ill fit. If Machado were now in the past tense, I would certainly condemn heartless Mother Nature for taking him. But here on the water, "almost" doesn't count. I wouldn't give Machado's near demise another thought.

Our best day of fishing and worst of weather was followed by the opposite, which put a slight damper in my optimistic view of coming out a winner by putting a trip together against all odds. The fishing had slowed throughout the tiny fleet, so there was no reason for me to go hunting for a better spot or attempting to squeeze into fishier water between two of my comrades. Everyone was locked in irons—we all had sails up but were making little or no headway. I knew from past experience that the fish would start actively feeding again and that we just needed to keep throwing the gear out into what looked like promising water. The frustrating hours spent chasing bitter ends of part-offs persisted and came to their peak on one particularly long day. We had been diligent about cutting chafed or weak spots out of the line as we hauled each day. But we couldn't get rid of everything that looked suspect, or we'd have nothing left to fish with. The weather was back to what I call half sloppy—just sort of miserable, and coupled with the main line's refusal to stay together it had us once again on deck well after the sun went down and conceding that we'd be forced to take yet another night off. The other boats were preparing to begin their sets as we tied back in to a bitter end of line found just at the edge of total darkness. I began to haul "braille" fashion, which I was becoming pretty good at, and prayed that we could get the remaining three miles aboard without another problem.

The wind seemed to have dropped out at sunset, leaving a long, low swell that rocked the *Seahawk* gently. The absence of howling wind, pounding waves, and sloshing water resulted in a pronounced, relative silence now. A quiet crew usually indicates an unhappy crew. I couldn't blame them for being as sullen as they appeared. How much longer would they endure this? I wondered. Not much had gone right this trip. Some of the problems we had brought on ourselves, like my arrest. But others seemed to be thrown at us from the sky without warning or justification. At each fleeting instance when our situation seemed a little brighter, a dark cloud had appeared and totally shut out any light. It was as if fate were teasing us. Every time I'd said, "Things can't get any worse," they did. I untied my hood, a symbolic gesture rightly interpreted by the crew as signifying that a hard-won battle was over. The night was nearly peaceful, and I could hear and be heard without shouting. The men were all lined up at the rail behind me, waiting for the next slack leader to hit my fist. I knew that we hadn't caught many fish today, but rather than ignoring the fact or pretending not to be concerned, I asked Machado for a tally. "Eight fish, Linny. Maybe a grand. Hopefully, we'll catch a couple nice ones on this end." But his tone was less than hopeful. I figured we were now at the halfway point of our trip, and we had only about eight thousand pounds of fish aboard. The crew was well aware of the dim prospect of making money at this rate.

Eight was the lowest of the trip. It felt bad to hear confirmation of what I'd suspected of the tally. I refused to register the disappointment of our dismal catch, knowing that things could and would turn around. We just needed to stay positive and keep plugging. We couldn't compete with the other boats; we weren't in their league. Although we were fine in our pounds-caught-per-hook-fished, the shortage of line and floats prohibited us from fishing more than half of what the other boats were able to set out each night. But I knew that we could still beat the extreme odds that seemed to keep stacking up against us. I had unplugged the remote VHF speaker long before, so that my crew wouldn't hear the discouraging reports around us. When no one is catching, there's a tendency to lose faith and yearn for home. My stubborn streak was never as wide as it had become during this three-week stint aboard the *Seahawk*. We were in a slump and would slug it out—no matter what. Machado leaned with both hands on the rail between Archie and me. He stared into the darkness as if searching for a buoy we hadn't parted off yet. "Hey, Arch," he said softly as he handed a leader aft to Timmy, "this ain't lookin' good, man. This is a disaster."

This was the first time I'd heard one of my crew refer to our situation as what it was shaping up to be—a disaster. I assumed they'd been discussing our missteps and misfortune in my absence; crews always do that. I prepared a pep talk in my mind to follow whatever lamenting came from the guys in response to Machado's leading remark. I would bolster their confidence by telling them about trips that would make this one look like a real winner. I would assure them that we still had bait and fuel for another ten sets if need be. The fish would bite when the moon reached its first quarter phase. We were in control of our paychecks and our destiny. I would tell them that we were in this together and we would buck up and we would be fine. I honestly believed it. They would, too. Now it seemed that everyone was waiting for Archie to respond. I wondered if Arch was still confident that we could pull it off or if he was ready to throw in the towel. He appeared to be thinking. Machado wasn't patient. "Come on, Arch, buddy. I need some pumping up. I am fuckin' discouraged. I've had it. How are we going to make any money out of this horror show?"

I was getting ready to jump in and save Arch before he could possibly join the ranks of despair. We didn't have much that was solid to pin faith or optimism to right now. To me this would be Archie's defining moment. Before I began what would have sounded like pleading for the guys to hang with me for a few more sets and promised them that things would turn around to our benefit and told them we'd come too far to give up now, Arch looked as though he had a revelation or an epiphany. His eyes grew wide. He held an index finger in the air, asking us all to pay attention. He smiled and said, "Merchandising." We remained silent as Archie thought a little more. I threw the boat out of gear to deal with a sharked-up leader but kept an ear on what Archie might add.

The next sound came from Timmy, who began laughing so hard he couldn't speak. His laugh was instantaneously contagious. I was basically laughing at Timmy laughing. Tears streamed down his beet-red cheeks, and he finally managed one word: "Merchandising?"

"Yeah, merchandising. You know, stuff to sell," Arch explained through a chuckle. "I'll start working on a marketing plan. We'll offer *Seahawk* lunch boxes. Kids love lunch boxes—they'll be big sellers."

Now Machado chimed in. "Lunch boxes are a great idea. We'll recommend a very unhealthy *Seahawk* diet—lots of stuffing and gravy. And when the kids pick up the boxes, the handles will fall off and the thermoses will leak."

Hiltz added, "But they'll come with a repair kit of two-part epoxy and a bungee cord. The kids will love that! And what about plastic swordfish? A few anyway. And lots of sharks! And an *Eagle Eye II* boat, complete with towline to attach to the *Seahawk*'s bow."

"Don't forget the action figures," said Timmy. "We'll offer an entire line of talking dolls dressed in oilskins and boots. We'll start with the Archie doll, because it was your idea," he said as he pushed an imaginary button in the middle of Archie's back.

"Timmmaay!" Arch yelled in his best imitation of himself.

Shrieks of laughter filled the deck. Archie pulled an imaginary string from Machado's back, and Machado responded immediately: "This boat is sucking the life out of me."

Machado in turn pushed Timmy's button, which resulted in, "I fixed it. I think we're all right now."

The Hiltz doll had a string *and* a button: "All I want to do is catch fish" and "I quit."

When Hiltz pulled the string from the Linda Greenlaw doll, she yelled, "Put the fuckin' door in!" Hiltz pulled my string a number of times, and I yelled with each pull, much to the delight of my crew. We carried on with this wonderful foolishness until the end beeper came aboard and the fish tally remained at eight. There are things out of our control, but attitude is not one of them. I had never loved and respected any crew member more than I did Archie right then. He was indeed the gem I knew he would be.

Our next day of fishing was equally bad. I recorded ten fish in my logbook. But the weather had improved greatly, and we celebrated quietly in only one part-off and got the gear back in time to set out with the fleet—a true *Seahawk* triumph. Now all we needed was for the fish to "turn on" and really start biting. The crew had become vocal in their support of my opinion that we must stick it out and that we would be successful in the end. The guys began speaking with some affection about the boat, saying that she had character and that she really was a good sea boat, meaning that she was quite comfortable and that they felt safe aboard her. We were in control of our destiny, and nothing could keep us down. Even Machado was optimistic and feeling good about our having overcome so many obstacles, and he really believed we'd have a decent trip against all odds.

I realized that I hadn't heard the guys refer to our vessel as the *Shithawk* in some time until the next evening, when she regained that name. I was scoping out the break and just about ready to give the guys the sign to toss the end buoy. Things were as good as they'd been all trip; fishing, mechanics, weather, and morale had finally all joined hands. Timmy scrambled up the stairs and said, "Dave got a real bad shock." I could tell from his tone that there was a sense of urgency and that he wasn't talking about static electricity. I threw the boat out of gear and followed Timmy back down to the deck, where the guys were huddled around Hiltz, who was sitting on a cooler. His oil pants were around his ankles, and he cradled his arms against his chest. Hiltz's eyes were glazed and unfocused. They were red, and goop seeped from their corners. Snot ran from his nose, dripping down into his mustache and beard.

Archie was holding Dave's shoulders and speaking softly to him, "Stay with me, Dave. You're going to be fine. You got a bad shock." Hiltz could only moan in reply. I took his pulse and was relieved to find a very strong one. I would be lying to say I wasn't terrified. Hiltz just looked so pathetic. When I asked what had happened, I learned that he had simply tried to turn on the deck lights. He apparently got zapped, causing his muscles to tighten so that he couldn't release his grip on the hot switch. It wasn't until he lost consciousness and fell to the deck that his hand was torn from the current, releasing him from the 110-volt stream. Within a few minutes, Hiltz was speaking, but not very coherently. He repeatedly asked if we were fishing, in a voice that was faint and mumbling. His lack of focus and confused state scared me. He muttered that his arm hurt. His hand appeared to be discolored. He asked if he could go to sleep. While Archie held Dave up and kept him somewhat alert, I ran to the wheelhouse to make some calls for advice.

My first call was to Scotty over the SSB radio. I've always had great respect for the captain of the *Eagle Eye II* and considered him as smart and knowledgeable on a wide range of topics as anyone I'd ever known. Scotty calmed my nerves by sharing his opinion that a shock of 110 volts was not lethal and that in his experience the victim was always fine given some time. Although I was glad to hear that, I was still very nervous. What if Scotty had never seen anyone who was shocked as severely as Dave had been? I picked up the satellite phone and by some miracle was able to get through to my friend Simon. He's a doctor. Granted, a retired orthopedic surgeon, but a doctor nonetheless. He'd know what to do, I thought. Simon reassured me by pretty much concurring with Scotty. He asked about Dave's pulse and said that it would be okay to allow him to go to sleep. He warned that Hiltz could possibly feel as if he'd been run over by a truck when he came around, but other than that, Simon thought he would be fine.

I hurried back to the deck to relay this information. Hiltz looked even worse now than he had five minutes earlier. He was babbling, his eyes were rolling around in their sockets, and he appeared sort of half poached. I watched him for a few minutes and discussed options. I wondered who would take the rap for an electrocution. It was an impossible leap to say that fate had anything to do with it. The guys were already cursing the makeshift and last-minute electrical work done to get us off the dock, and once again we were the proud captain and crew of the *Shithawk*. Finally I asked the guys to get Hiltz to his bunk so that we could set the gear. This was met with some hard looks but no words. I felt pretty coldhearted, but I had to believe that Hiltz would be fine. Besides, what could we have done if he wasn't? We were here to fish, and that's what we would do. At the risk of sounding paranoid, this was just the most recent of strikes against us and our ability to get a paying trip. We had to persevere.

The men reluctantly helped Hiltz to his bunk, where they tucked him in and promised to take turns checking on him throughout the five-hour setting process. I thought Archie might cry, he was so upset that one of his shipmates had been nearly fried. But the guys set the gear shorthanded, and I got several intermittent reports regarding Hiltz's snoring and turning over in his bunk, and I took some mind-easing looks myself to ensure that he was indeed breathing. When the end buoy splashed into the black wake behind the boat and the guys peeled off oil clothes and prepared for a nap, Hiltz arose from his deathbed and asked what had happened. He was still quite bleary but seemed to understand what he was told, although he had no recollection of being partially electrocuted.

The next day was brilliant. It was haulback number ten, and things really came together. We tallied twenty-five fish, and nice ones at that! We again retrieved the gear in a timely fashion allowing us to set it right back out. This was the way I remembered swordfishing to be. Timmy had the mechanical problems at bay. The weather was splendid. The crew rejoiced in what seemed to be our beating another major obstacle. Not even electrocution could keep us down! Hiltz was sore, but not of spirit. All the muscles on his right side from his hand to his buttocks were extremely weak, but this didn't keep him from working as hard as ever. Mother Nature, mechanical problems, poor fishing, the gods— there was nothing we couldn't take to the mat. The wild sea had been tamed to a docile subservience. The sun had been forced out of hiding. The guys were elated that we were pulling fish aboard with some frequency and a paycheck was within reach. None of us could imagine anything we hadn't yet encountered in the way of deterrence. We were cocky in our posture of nobody or nothing being a match for us. We were tough and callused. I hauled faster and harder than ever. Machado's knife went through fish like it was silk. We were finally looking like a real, experienced team. We clicked. There was just nothing left to get in our way. We all shared an attitude of "Bring it on!"

For the first time since we made our very first set twelve days before, I didn't have to tell the crew to get bait out of the freezer. They seemed enthusiastic about fishing now. Today's haul had landed another three thousand pounds of the healthiest fish we'd seen yet, and we had another six sets to make. I estimated a total of close to twenty thousand in the hold and knew that forty thousand was well within reach at our present rate. The moon was just beyond its first quarter. The weather gurus predicted nothing but light and variable winds in the foreseeable future. I knew the importance of staying on our game at this point. We couldn't let our guard down. We couldn't get too comfortable. There was no room for mistakes. Neither fate, nor luck, nor the gods would take credit for the pulling off of such an impossible feat as we were so close to doing. It was easy to believe that we were the center of the universe. All revolved around us. Every act aboard the *Seahawk* was so painstakingly deliberate. We would take nothing for granted.

"*Seahawk, Eagle Eye II.* On here, Linda? Come on." The ring in Scotty's voice indicated that he'd also had a great day. I'd learned that the telling detail was in the tone of his signature "Come on." I was quick to answer my friend and knew he would be pleased to hear a positive report from me, too. My crew and I had set our mark on catching half of what Scotty did each day, and we considered that amount something to celebrate. We figured he had twice the boat and twice the gear and was the high-liner of the fleet. So if we could just catch 50 percent of Scotty's act, we had nothing to be ashamed of. I waited patiently to hear a number from Scotty in anticipation of my own boast of twenty-eight fish aboard the *Seahawk* today. I never dreamed that twenty-eight fish would feel so good. It felt like one of the hundred-fish days enjoyed aboard the *Hannah Boden.* Scotty was interrupted mid-transmission, right after his report of forty-six fish, and excused himself, promising to get right back to me.

Wow, I marveled as I waited for Scotty to come back on the radio, we had done better than I thought with our small boat and our short string of gear. Quite respectable indeed. And the sharks hadn't bothered us. And we had only parted off once in the entire haulback. Life was good and showed signs of getting even better. I was eager to tell Scotty how our day had gone, as I was sure he was weary of all my bad news and perpetual problems and my asking for troubleshooting advice and medical consults and . . . If I were Scotty, I'd be quite hesitant to answer me on the radio, I chuckled to myself.

Finally, after what seemed like a very long time, Scotty returned. His voice wasn't quite as chipper as it had been. "Hey, Linda. That was Malcolm on my satellite phone. He's been trying your phone, but no dice. He asked me to pass along this message: You are to be at the dock in Bay Bulls, Newfoundland, Monday morning. No ifs, ands, or buts about it." I felt as though I'd been popped with a pin—totally deflated. I couldn't even figure out when Monday was, or why my boss had shut me down midtrip. I was stunned into silence, and then Scotty added, "You would have to leave now to get to the dock Monday."

This was confusing, a cruel joke you hope you've misunderstood. My thoughts were awash for a few seconds while I processed what Scotty had relayed to me. It was totally unheard of in my vast experience to be called back to the dock before completing a trip. I hardly dared tell my crew. Could I possibly ignore the order? Could I thumb my nose at Malcolm and say, "We're staying out with your shit boat until we finish this friggin' trip"? I had, in the past, been ordered to stay out. I had never been ordered, nor even been made to feel welcome, to come in before the hold was full. Everyone aboard any boat always wants to go in. But not us, not now, not this way. I thanked Scotty for the message without ever telling him about our twenty-eight fish. God, I wanted to stay out and finish what we'd started and suffered through. I didn't want an excuse for failure. Of course I wanted to succeed. Or if I couldn't do that, I wanted to fail on my own terms. I wanted no excuses for failure.

To disobey Malcolm's order was within my control. Malcolm was an old man and fifteen hundred miles away. But the reality of the fact that all I had invested financially in this venture was a pair of rubber boots weighed heavily. Maybe *I* wasn't out here for the money, but my crew needed to be compensated. If I bolted, they might never get paid.

But for all my concern for the crew, my real thoughts were about number one, me. Where was the young, feisty captain of my past? Was this to be the metaphor for my middle age? When "they" call you to the dock, you're done. Ouch, I thought. This could be the biggest cop-out of my life. The culmination of nearly thirty years of life on the water boiled down to what I had to prove in this outing. This had not turned out to be the noted comeback I'd hoped for.

I had, however, confirmed one suspicion. The renegade in me had faded in the past decade. Jimmy Buffett, step aside. *This* pirate was looking at fifty. My life had changed. I had established a life on land. The sea was no longer my only option. I reluctantly turned the *Seahawk* toward the dock. I had learned a few things over the years I'd spent dangling hooks that pertained to life on land or sea, and one of them was this: There are some things out of my control. And "seaworthy" was no longer the only adjective in my vocabulary.

Epilogue

hy we were ordered to the dock was baffling at the time, and the ten months that have passed since haven't produced a satisfactory answer. The boss was reasoning that, historically, the price of sword has always been at its highest annual point following the full moon in November. So, in theory, if we were able to land this trip, return to the fishing grounds immediately, and land with a second trip during or after the next moon, we would have been rolling in dough. However, there is a very good explanation for the historic price spike in early winter. It's a function of supply and demand. There are no fish to catch. It doesn't matter how high the price is if you have nothing to sell. Swordfish migrate, and sometime between mid-October and the first of November they split, leaving the Grand Banks like tourists exiting Maine after Labor Day. They vanish. Poof—gone. And they do not return until the next season, which begins in late spring. We were ordered to unload in Newfoundland on the twentieth of October. I was nervous that by the time we turned the boat around (unloaded, cleaned, and resupplied) and got back to the fishing grounds, the proverbial fat lady could be finishing her encore and we'd be setting out in an empty ocean.

Being the totally compliant goody-goody that I am, my crew and I landed in Bay Bulls, Newfoundland, as ordered by Malcolm and unloaded just shy of twenty thousand pounds of gorgeous swordfish. Offloading fish in small-town Newfoundland is unlike any such process I have witnessed in Boston or New Bedford, Massachusetts, or Portland, Maine. The whole town gets in on the action in one way or another—some folks stopping by to welcome us while others manned the scale or the forklift or shoveled ice or built boxes in which to ship the fish. Because of the small population, the unloading of swordboats is good part-time employment for quite a large segment, including women and children. Better for them than for me, alas. Our timing, my nemesis of late, was perfectly awful, and in the growing tradition of all good Americans I can blame the bad economy for the rock-bottom price of three bucks per pound that we received for our catch.

Machado had the good sense to bail, and he headed home to his real job at Boston Sword and Tuna. I was fortunate to replace Machado with a young fisherman from my hometown of Isle au Haut, Nate Clark. Getting a man to Newfoundland on short notice took time. After five days ashore that echoed most of the hardship that had preceded them at sea, we pounded our way back to the fishing grounds in the most unwelcoming of weather, which is typical of the end of October. In the best of faith, we had high hopes of capturing that big price Malcolm spoke of, and we all had dollar signs in our eyes, knowing that we'd left decent fishing just one week before. We prayed that we would put a small trip aboard before the season came to an abrupt end, which it did before we did. I guess the fish hadn't taken the same economics course that Malcolm had.

On the bright side was Nate Clark. Nate was a real asset in his hustle and enthusiasm to learn the business of catching sword-fish, and he was like the clichéd breath of fresh air among his dogged and aged captain and shipmates. Nate sparked a little life into our team for five sets, until the fish disappeared with the fleet, and we soon followed, game over.

I waved good-bye to the *Seahawk* with a contradiction of emotions that included sadness and elation. An overwhelming sense of good riddance was tapped on the shoulder by a very shy submission that whispered, "Your swordfishing days are over." But sorrow was soon lost in the rearview mirror as I reentered my life ashore. My homecoming to Isle au Haut was unlike any I remembered from the past, in that I actually felt like I had come home. Previous returns to hard land from sea had been just that—hard. So it was easier this time, but the tension was still there. The sea tugged constantly at my shirttail when I was ashore; it felt like the tide pulling me back out. And that tide ran the hardest on the Fourth of July.

Forever my favorite holiday, the Fourth this year was at my place. My mother—who's a great cook and a cookbook author—had organized the menu and had done the majority of the cooking, assigning my siblings and me each a dish to prepare. We borrowed tables from the town hall to seat all twenty-two guests. I sat with my back to the front yard and faced the view of Penobscot Bay so I wouldn't have to see the cowlicks my lawn had developed. I'd been fully immersed for eight months in my comfortable routine of writing and fishing a few lobster traps. Sarai was home from school for the summer, Simon was coming and going, my nephews were living with me while their parents commuted back and forth to work, and my last sword trip was slowly evolving from a nightmare to a good story. Then the phone rang.

"Hi, Linny. It's Arch. I know of a boat in need of a captain. Are you in?"

The fear that I had just caught my last fish was one that I overcame every single time we threw lines off the dock in the twenty years I fished for sword. Can I rise to the battle once more? Is my love of the sea still great enough for me to risk my pride in my ability to catch fish or my confidence to withstand anything? The merging of two separate worlds began when I hired friends from my land life to go to sea with me. I had never done that before. It just seems like a Grand Canyon–size divide I must cross to go between my lives at sea and ashore. I'm so comfy and safe here at home. But I know that I really thrive on the life of wild adventure at sea. I'm weaving these two worlds together, and it's neither seamless nor totally comfortable.

Somewhere in the midst of all this contemplation of yet another return to blue-water fishing and the lifestyle it requires, Hurricane Bill charged up the East Coast. Glad to be at home, and not fifteen hundred miles from the dock, I thought I was relieved to be living the storm vicariously through the plate-glass windows of my cozy home. On the evening news, I learned that fifteen people watching the surf smash against the shore at Thunder Hole on Mount Desert Island were swept from the rocks and carried out to sea by a rogue wave. A seven-year-old girl was killed. It made me think. In twenty years of offshore fishing, I have never lost a man to the sea. Perhaps the divide between land and sea isn't as wide as I once believed it was. And maybe I can have both.

Tim Palmer is now on the water in a number of capacities, mostly captaining one of his two commercial vessels and delivering large sportfishing boats between the United States and Mexico. At the end of our trip, I was asked if I would ever try again, to which I replied that I would not go offshore without Timmy. And I meant it. I hope he doesn't make me eat those words, but I suppose he will at some point, because I have no intention of passing on the right opportunity, and Timmy is too sharp to subject himself to this type of torture again.

I see my friend, neighbor, and former crew member Dave Hiltz almost daily here on the island. He's currently fishing the lobsters pretty hard, manufacturing custom knives, and planning his much-beloved hunting trips.

Archie Jost is home in Stuart, Florida, where he will never retire from selling hot tubs, fishing, and dreaming up plans for turning a dollar. We are both still scratching our heads about our joint decision to take the *Seahawk* to the Grand Banks in the state she was in. Arch has always been a pal, but it wasn't until I saw him in action in real adversity that I fully understood what a truly great man he is.

As for me, I'm fishing a few lobster traps, doing some boat charters in conjunction with the Inn at Isle au Haut, starting up a herring-seining business with some fishing buddies—Omega Four, Inc.—and sharing a home and guidance with the seventeen-year-old and beautiful Sarai. In my free time I roam the island with my nephews Aubrey and Addison and my friend Simon.

My scrape with the Canadian authorities finally came to a conclusion on May 25, seven months after I got busted. I traveled to Newfoundland to stand trial with great confidence that my "due diligence" defense afforded me by Canadian law would clear my good name. But no one facing these particular charges in Canada has ever been acquitted, and I was not to be the first. My sentence was a fine of thirty-five thousand dollars plus our catch. I have always paid for my indiscretions, but this one was a little more costly than most. My detractors accuse me of intentionally crossing the line for publicity or for a book opportunity, to which I say bullshit—not my style. It happened. I have now written about it. So call me a pragmatist. But don't call me an opportunist.

The combination of a shaky boat, lack of gear and electronics, the worst economy ever, poor decision making on behalf of my boss, and a rusty captain proved to be lethal on payday, which came nine months after we disembarked from our beloved ship. The settlement sheet shows a personal debit of $787, a number that puts an exclamation point at the end of my fifty-two-day epic disaster. In hindsight I realize that I was naïve in my eagerness to get back into the business of swordfishing. I do have standards—even if they're low—and I owe it to my crew in the future to see that some minimum demands are met. Did I say future? I guess not everything has changed in my time ashore. . . .

So when Archie called, I rose to the bait. It looks like I'll be heading out to sea again. I guess I find it impossible to say no when somebody says, "Let's go fishing!"

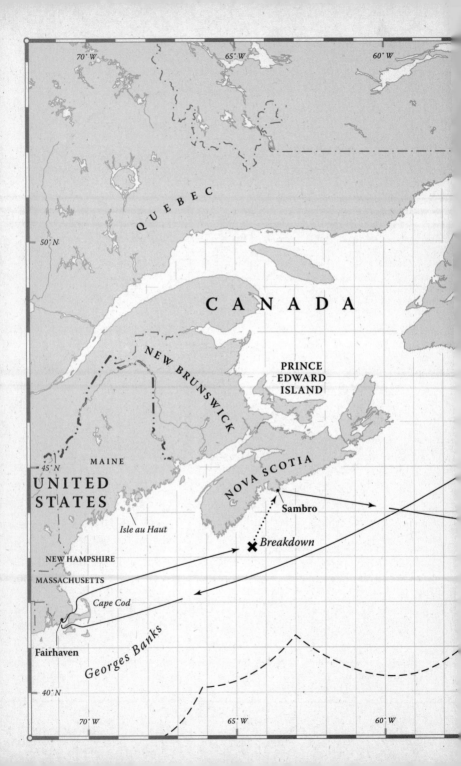

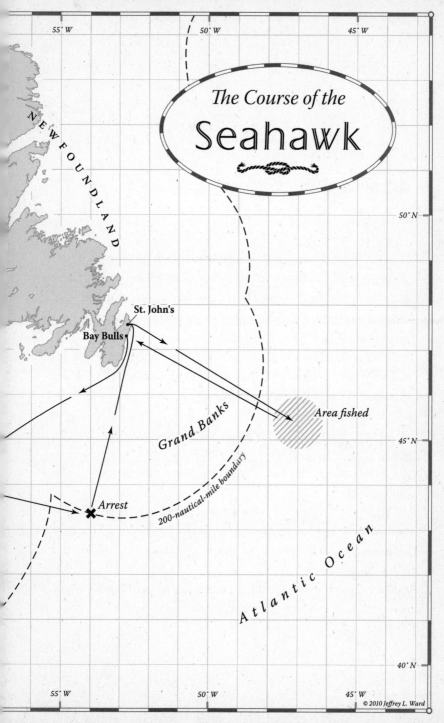

The Course of the Seahawk

NEWFOUNDLAND

St. John's

Bay Bulls

Area fished

Grand Banks

Arrest

200-nautical-mile boundary

Atlantic Ocean

55° W   50° W   45° W

50° N

45° N

40° N

55° W   50° W   45° W

© 2010 Jeffrey L. Ward

Acknowledgments

I am excited and proud and, yes, grateful for this new venture with Viking Penguin. Thanks to so many people for taking a leap of faith and signing me on. To name a few: Clare Ferraro, Carolyn Coleburn, Louise Braverman, Nancy Sheppard, Bruce Giffords, Maggie Riggs—and, of course, my editor, Wendy Wolf.

Thanks once again to my literary agent, Stuart Krichevsky, for his guidance and patience throughout. Thanks also to Shana Cohen and Kathryne Wick of the Stuart Krichevsky Literary Agency for their help in so many areas.

Special thanks to Will Schwalbe, who agreed to be my "editor for life."

Thanks to my friends Dr. and Mrs. David Bahnson for help in proofreading.

Thanks to Jim Budi and Malcolm MacLean for the opportunity to captain the mighty *Seahawk*. Thanks also to Tom Beers and the crew at Original Productions and the Discovery Channel for making this trip possible.

I send great and many thanks to my friends and family, whose moral support, encouragement, and love mean so much.